THE BLACK FLAG
OVER CARMARTHEN

The Black Flag over Carmarthen

Peter J.R. Goodall

ISBN: 0-86381-966-4

Cover design: Sian Parri

First published in 2005 by
Gwasg Carreg Gwalch, 12 Iard yr Orsaf, Llanrwst,
Wales LL26 0EH
☎ 01492 642031 ▤ 01492 641502
✆ books@carreg-gwalch.co.uk   website: www.carreg-gwalch.co.uk

for
my wife Pauline,
my children
Andrew, Wayne and Amanda,
and grandchildren,
my mother Audrey and my father Douglas James Goodall
who sadly passed away before my second book went to press.

Acknowledgements

I would like to thank the following for their invaluable help in the preparation of this book.

Once again my special thanks to my wife, Pauline for her continued bullying and cajoling me through the writing process and her many hours of proofreading!

The Governor and Staff at HMP Swansea. Retired Senior Officer Glyn Lewis for the use of photographs and memorabilia from his grandfather, Warder James Hughes and grandmother, Matron Mary Jane Hughes. James and Mary Hughes remained at the gaol as caretakers until the gaol was finally demolished. Steve Fielding, author of *The Hangman's Record*, who provided the profile of some of the executioners who officiated at Carmarthen Gaol hangings.

Carmarthenshire County Museum
Carmarthenshire County Archives
Swansea Public Library
Carmarthen Public Library
West Glamorgan Archives
Carmarthen Journal and South Wales Evening Post for their
    continued support and advice

Whilst every effort was used to trace the authors of articles used in this book it was not possible in every case. I would be pleased to receive any information which has necessarily been omitted here.

Peter J.R. Goodall

Contents

Preface 8

Chapter One 9

Chapter Two 14

Chapter Three 27

Chapter Four 37

Chapter Five 44

Chapter Six 105

Source of Reference 108

Preface

My first book, 'For Whom The Bell Tolls, A Century of Executions', employed only about a third of the work researched. The original manuscript contained many more facts on the early history of the penal system employed in the 17th and 18th century. However much had to be edited along the way. That book, with its theme of executions at Swansea and the history of Swansea gaol inspired me to look at other gaols in the principality, and in particular Carmarthen Gaol. The British penal system underwent many reforms and much of it was due to the reformists, people like John Howard and Elizabeth Fry who between them brought about many of the changes that are still, employed to this day.

Carmarthen with its history of drunkenness, violence, and debt was home to not one gaol but two. One of them served the Borough and the other the County. Both performed different functions. It was in these gaols that Howard entered and found that the conditions employed were below any acceptable level. The 'Lower Orders' of Carmarthen were proud people and unlike today's society, who will steal for profit, and to fund further criminal activity, the criminals of these early days stole to survive. Most of the inhabitants of Carmarthen were honest men and women, too preoccupied with the day-to-day business of making an honest living or merely surviving. As in today's society, it is the minority, who figure prominently in breaking the law and it is these, who would end up before the courts to await their fate. However, the punishment for such offences was high. Deportation, execution, flogging, incarceration all played a major part in the punishment meted out by the courts. No two offences brought the same sentence. With some 200 offences carrying the death penalty in the early 1700s, the price for crime could be high. It was the gaols that housed the criminals sent by the courts and many a man, woman and child, started and ended their life in these dark dismal places. The lucky ones were deported whilst the unlucky could be executed or remain in custody for many years, surviving on the good will of the unscrupulous gaoler and the town folk.

This is the story of the gaols and the people who ended their lives on the various scaffolds. This book covers the history of the town and County gaols of Carmarthen and the changes and amalgamations that took place. Unlike Swansea, where the gaol still plays a prominent part in the maintenance of law and order, in 1922 Carmarthen lost the gaol with all the remaining prisoners being transferred to either Swansea or Cardiff and the gaol closed its doors for the last time. This is their story.

Peter J.R. Goodall
2005

Chapter One

Early History of Carmarthen Gaol

The castle at Carmarthen dates from around 1094, when the name Rhyd y Gors is first used. By 1105, the annals refer to Carmarthen by name and it is then that the Norman, William Fitz Baldwin built the first Norman castle on the present site. Certainly, around the 12th and 13th centuries the castle was rebuilt on many occasions following the turbulent struggles between the Welsh and the English. One of the earliest recorded captures and destruction of the castle was by Llywelyn the Great in 1215, and it was after this period that the castle underwent a major reconstruction. William Marshal the younger earl of Pembroke, re-captured the castle in 1223 and it is believed that he was instrumental in providing the massive stone defences and the original moat.

The history of a gaol at Carmarthen can be traced back to mid 1532, when Walter Devereux (Lord Ferrers) reported to the Kings minister Thomas Cromwell that Lleuan ap Ricard and a monk named Dan Rychard were coining money in the monastery. They were arrested and placed in Carmarthen Castle. In the mid 1600's William Jones who later become the leader of the new Baptist cause known as 'Rhydwilym', was held as a prisoner in Carmarthen Castle gaol. The gaol is also mentioned in the Corporation proceedings of 1551 and continued to be regularly mentioned up to 1755.

In 1582 an order was made:

If the Mayor or Justices of the peace, shall commit any person to ward, the bailiff shall not enlarge any such person from the ward without special licence of the Mayor.

In 1724 the Order Book recorded

That the town gaol was to be repaired out of the town rents.

Clearly, the gaol was becoming an important aspect of town life in Carmarthen. The castle was converted into the county gaol in 1789 and later extended in 1869 to take up the whole of the open space within the grounds of what had been known as The Castle Green. On the site now stands the council offices and this building has all but destroyed what was an important military location and prominent setting in the defence of the region. It was during this period of reconstruction that Carmarthen lost most of what remained of the medieval castle. John Nash the architect finished what Llywelyn the Great, Owain Glyndŵr and many more had failed to do.

With the centuries of neglect, one of the most impressive, strongest and most important of the Welsh castles has now all but vanished. The extension of the Castle Green has meant that the remains of the castle were incorporated into the prison construction. With the closure of the prison in 1922 and demolition in 1938 to make way for the County Hall, very little remained to remind us of the harsh times on Castle Hill, when in earlier days it was known as *CURSITORS FIELD*. This is described in the Carmarthenshire Antiquity as:

A loss to the historian but a boon to generations of malefactors and unfortunates.

John Howard

John Howard, the famous penal reformer, had close connections with Carmarthen gaol. Born on 2nd September, 1726 in Hackney London he is known as an English philanthropist and reformer in the field of penology. In 1742 at the age of 16 he inherited his father's wealth and began to travel Europe. On his return to Bedfordshire he became the High Sheriff and as part of his duties he visited Bedford gaol and was appalled to find that the sanitation was way below any acceptable standard at the time. He also found that gaolers were not salaried officials but depended on fees extracted from the prisoners, he also found many of the prisoners in the gaol had been acquitted by the courts but the unscrupulous gaoler kept them in gaol until such time as they had paid 'the discharge fee'. He continued to travel the country widely, touring Scotland, Ireland, Wales, England and on the continent France, Netherlands, Germany and Switzerland often visiting local prisons as he went. He found that in all cases the poor sanitation and the ill treatment of prisoners was rife throughout the penal system and as a result on his return to England he persuaded the House of Commons in 1774 to pass two Acts. The essence of these were:

1. *That discharged persons should be set at liberty in open court and that discharge fees should be abolished.*

2. *That Justices should be required to see to the health of prisoners.*

Years later however Howard complained that the acts were not being observed and that the unscrupulous gaolers were still demanding '*a discharge fee*'.

Carmarthen, Borough and County Gaols

It was in 1774 that Howard first visited Carmarthen and here he found that the town boasted of two gaols, one located in the remains of the castle and the other the Borough Gaol located at the East Gate, also known as the Prisoners Gate, in the area between King Street and Nott Square. It was in this gaol that the debtors of the town were locked-up. Passers by would often see baskets being lowered from the windows with pleas coming from within the gaol, '*Remember the poor debtors*'.

Howard found that the conditions in the two gaols mirrored each other. He described them as being squalid and dilapidated. He found the two old gaols were in a very poor condition structurally, sanitation was non-existent and the accommodation being little more than small, damp mud-floored cells, with no drinking water. The condemned dungeon was cold and very damp, with water running down the walls. The gaolers lived far from the gaols and received no pay, existing on the *discharge fee* and other tolls extracted from the prisoners or their families and friends.

The prisoners were not allowed furniture, not even a stool. Men, women and children were herded together in the same room. With rape a common occurrence in the gaol, eventually the women and children were moved but is was still some years before the rooms were locked. There was no glass in the windows, no fuel allowed even in the coldest period of winter, and very little food. If they had no friends to provide the necessaries of sustenance, they had to depend upon charity, and the tender mercy of the '*Poor-Law Guardians*' for daily bread and medicine when sick. Not even a drop of water was in reach of the wretched prisoners. Water could only be obtained when the Head Gaoler was present. This was not always the case, as he lived in a distant part of the town and so could not aid them even in an emergency. The gaolers had no scruples about oppressing those unfortunate individuals who were entrusted to their mercy. Disease was rife due to the poor sanitation. Personal cleanliness was a matter that never entered into anyone's thoughts.

Segregation of class was unheard of and the old and young were herded together irrespective of their crime. It is on record that an eleven-year-old girl was deprived of her supper for failing to pick her daily task of oakum and one year later she appears again for the same offence and received the same punishment. *(The task of oakum was to produce a caulking-fibre obtained by picking pieces of rope. It was mixed with pitch and the caulk was then used to stop up seams of ships.)*

A doctor only visited when absolutely necessary, and care for the spiritual welfare was never attended to; although there were provisions on the record books to record visits, none can be traced.

These conditions where common features in gaols of the 18th century and Carmarthen was no exception. On Howard's return to Carmarthen some 14 years later in May 1788, he found to his horror that conditions had not improved in either gaol. In fact, if anything conditions were worse. As a result, he was able to report to Parliament, no doubt armed with his knowledge of having visited many gaols in this country and abroad. *'That the Justices, Gentlemen, Clergy and Freeholders' of Carmarthenshire, together with the Mayor, Justices, Burgesses and inhabitants of Carmarthen begged that a Parliamentary Bill be brought in for the demolishing of the two gaols and that a new single gaol be built to serve the Borough and County.'*

Plans were submitted to Parliament for the reconstruction of Carmarthen Gaol. Parliament authorised and approved the plans and raised the money to defray the expense. With the construction of the new gaol, the East Gate was closed. However, the Corporation felt that they still needed a town gaol and in 1803 the Borough Order Book recorded that on 14th January the Corporation subscribed £400 towards the building of a new small town gaol or 'Lock-up', known as 'The Roundhouse'. Completed around 1810 on the 'Old Bowling Green', later the John Street and Cambrian Place area, a report in 1816 is believed to refer to the Borough Gaol:

Two strong doors be immediately provided, together with wrought iron bars for the windows, at the expense of the Corporation, for the lock-up house.

Debt, both in the Borough and the County gaols were the primary offences. Carmarthen Town had a reputation for drunkenness and brawls were frequent. Nevertheless, it never appeared to have a high crime rate, and even with the poor housing conditions, murder, theft and house-breakings were uncommon. Therefore, many who frequented the two gaols where held in custody for debt.

At the County Gaol, prisoners were employed on the tread wheel, which supplied the water to the gaol, in stone breaking for the surrounding roads, brick cleaning, cooking, sewing, clog making, cleaning and mending. At the Borough Gaol there was very little employment. Debtors were left to waste their days away. Accommodation was considered inferior to that at the County Gaol. It was described as consisting of four rooms and a yard for debtors but no day room. The average numbers of debtors confined were seven, but frequently there were between twelve and eighteen locked up at the same time.

As for the criminals of the County gaol, there were eight cells, with a day room and a yard for exercise. The women and children had the same accommodation as the men but the exercise yard had been converted into a garden for the gaoler.

Two years after visiting Carmarthen on 20th January, 1790 at the age of 64, whilst travelling in Russia to a military hospital in the Ukraine region, Howard contracted camp fever, and died of the disease.

It took many years for conditions in the penal system to improve. Elizabeth Fry born 1780, 10 years before the death of Howard, and no doubt inspired by Howard, carried on the work when she visited Newgate Gaol in 1813 for it was here that she saw the conditions that the females were living in. Like Howard she became well travelled and visited numerous prisons in France, Belgium, the Netherlands and Russia. Even while her health was failing in 1843 and no longer able to travel she kept in contact with the prisons right up to her death at Ramsgate on 12th October, 1845.

Following the intervention of John Howard, work on the new Carmarthen Gaol commenced in 1789 and completed in 1792. John Nash received the commission as the chief architect to build this new gaol; he later became famous for his design of Buckingham Palace and the Pavilion at Brighton.

Chapter 2

Prison, Punishment and Transportation

By the mid-nineteenth century, inspired by the earlier campaigns of John Howard and Elizabeth Fry, Victorian society was beginning to put its prison system into order on a more constructive footing. With New Prisons under construction all around the country and new standards of discipline and training being introduced, it was hoped that the convict would leave not simply 'punished', but reformed as well.

Over the centuries, many prisoners were transported to the colonies of America, Tasmania and Australia. In the 1700s over 200 offences for which the death sentence could be imposed, transportation was considered the alternative sentence. Many would volunteer to be the hangman in return for a lesser period of deportation. However, with disease rife on the rat infested, over crowded transport ships, for many death, was still the outcome.

It was after the American War of Independence around 1783 that America refused to receive any more of England's unwanted criminals. It was about this time that the hulk ships first appeared in the Thames. Used to house the country's most dangerous criminals and those awaiting transportation to the new colonies and penal deprivation of New South Wales and the notorious Botany Bay, the ships became feared by all who were sent on board to await their fate. Conditions were no better than the early transport ships that used to sail to America and again disease was rife on the rat infested floating gaols claiming many lives. Even those who survived the hulk ships would often perish on the long journey to their final destination in far away countries.

In the 1700s, the death penalty could be invoked for over 200 offences. By 1832, this had been reduced to 120 offences, and by 1837, the number had been further reduced to fifteen. After 1861, the death penalty was confined to offences of murder, treason, piracy with violence and arson in the Sovereign's vessels, arsenals and dockyards.

However, during the 17th and early 18th centuries, many murderers were able to cheat death with sentence of transportation to the colonies. Some were forced to go while others volunteered rather than face the executioner. There was yet another way to cheat death and that was with what became known as the 'Neck Verse'. If murderers could prove that they had been ordained as priests, then they could not be sent for trial in the secular courts and were set free. It was then possible for the murderer to be sent for trial in an ecclesiastical court. In medieval times all that was required to prove ordination was to prove literacy, and all that was required to prove literacy was to read, write or recite one verse of Psalm 51v1. Many murderers learnt the verse by heart to save their necks, before the ecclesiastical court:

Psalm 51 v1

Have mercy on me, O God,
According to your unfailing love;
According to your great compassion
Blot out my transgressions.
Wash away all my iniquity
And cleanse me from my sin.

Between 1752 and 1836 the sentence of death was carried out on the second day following the sentence of death unless it was a Sunday. In that case, the sentence was carried out on Monday. The exceptions to the rule were that the judge could respite the sentence of death while the condemned sought a reprieve. In some cases, the gallows were erected on the very spot where the murderous crime was committed; therefore, the building of the gallows could delay the execution. No executions ever took place on Good Friday. It was also customary for the body to be dissected before burial or hung in chains for all to see.

It was normal practice at the time for executions to take place in full public view. In Carmarthen, Babel Hill, Pensarn a mile from the town, was the location of the County executions, with another site near the Royal Oak Common at Johnstown, for town executions. At the end of the eighteenth century, it became clear that the long procession to the gallows allowed for no proper crowd control and in many cases the condemned man suffered the additional stress of having to walk the long distance through the jeering crowds to his death.

The last man to suffer the walk to Pensarn was Rees Thomas Rees in 1817. A new and safe place had to be found, and a new public gallows was erected inside the front wall of the County Gaol facing Spilman

Street. The last public execution in Carmarthen Gaol was that of David Evans in 1829. The crowds who came to witness the execution stretched along Spilman Street and as was the custom of the day, the dissected body was placed on display for all to see before burial within the prison grounds. It would be almost 60 years (1888) before Carmarthen was to witness another execution and by then it was no longer a public spectacle. The crowds who had flocked to these occasions were by now denied their 'Roman Holiday'.

Punishments, however remained harsh, The Daily Court Calendar as reported in the Cambrian on the 11th April, 1818, for the Counties of Pembroke and Haverfordwest makes interesting reading:

William Day, for stealing one cheese, one ham, butter and six shillings in silver, and Thomas Hughes for breaking into the offices of Henry Rees, Esq., and stealing shillings received the sentence of death.

Les Davies and John Edwards, for stealing cheese and butter from the dairy of the Rev W, Warlow received sentences of transportation for 14 years.

Mary Davies committed the same offence as the above and received a sentence of twelve months imprisonment. Whilst the co-accused, Joss Davies, for receiving the above property, knowing it to be stolen, was sentenced to 14 years transportation.

Stephen Williams and James Fountain, for producing forged currency were each sentenced to transportation for 14 years.

William Butler, for stealing from the pantry of Mr Caleb Evans, of the Parish of St Mary, Pembroke, two hams, two cheeks of bacon, several pounds of butter, various articles of wearing apparel from the stable of Mr Henry Hicks, of the Parish of Whitchurch, were ordered to be imprisoned for twelve months, and fined one shilling.

Bristol Gazette 1818
A man named Alford, a former gamekeeper, returned to his native country from Botany Bay. It was recorded at the time that some 28 years (1790) before he had been transported to Botany Bay for forging two receipts, the total amount under ten shillings, he had been sentenced to death, however he was reprieved and was transported to Botany Bay for life. Whilst at Botany Bay he came to the attention of the Governor and was employed as the Governors gardener for many years. Whilst in the employment of the Governor, he petitioned the Governor for leave to return to his native

country. It is on record that the Governor had expressed a great interest in his aged gardener and as he had always conducted himself well, the Governor therefore granted the petition. Alford had been transported in 1790 at the age of 53. When he returned on Sunday 15th March, 1818, he was 81 years old. However the journey had proved too much for the feeble old man and he died on Thursday 19th March, 1818, in the arms of his wife surrounded by his family.

The Treadmill

The treadmill at Carmarthen was located in the southwest corner close to the site of a well, overlooking Coracle Way and Little Bridge Street. Constructed in 1833 and in operation on 20th April, 1833, according to the records of William Spurrell it was used as a form of occupational therapy. Its design was simple: a symmetrical drum about six feet in diameter with rows of steps on its outside surface. Some treadmills were fitted with a braking system, others revolved, through a series of cogs and wheels, against weights. The end result was the same in both cases, providing pressure for the prisoner to work against. As he stepped onto the drum it began to revolve under his weight, and he would have to keep climbing-on-the spot in order to maintain his position. Prisoners worked a morning and an afternoon session, each of three hours with five minutes rest every quarter of an hour. By the end of the day, they would have travelled 2193 ft per hour and climbed over nine thousand feet – twice the height of Ben Nevis. The prison treadmill was used to provide power to pump water from the well to the tanks, in the roof.

The Crank

The treadmill, used as a form of exercise and occupational therapy served a purpose but the other form of punishment at prisons like Carmarthen was 'The Crank', it was completely demoralising and soul destroying. At least on the tread wheel you left the confines of your cell, the crank was part of the cell. The crank comprised a large box, fitted to the wall, or to the floor and filled with sand and gravel. A large handle, similar to those on an 'old mangle' projected from the side, with a paddle inside. This had to be pushed through the sand. The number of times the handle was turned was dictated by the warder. A 'SCREW' on the side which, when turned produced additional pressure on the handle. The tasks set on this machine would be 10,000 to 12,000 per day. It was usual to make a prisoner perform many revolutions in order to obtain his meals, i.e., 1,000 before breakfast, 5,000 before lunch and so on. It was from this period the nickname 'SCREW' was given to 'Prison Warders', who would tighten the pressure making it harder for the prisoner to turn the handle.

A Royal Commission appointed in the 1870's to look into cruel punishment discovered that at one gaol a man had only eaten nine meals in 21 days because he had failed to complete the number of revolutions ordered by the staff. It was to prevent such maltreatment and to establish an acceptable uniform discipline throughout the country that the Prison Act of 1878 was passed.

Gaolers Journal

Official records are often brief and to the point. Yet the Gaolers Journal and the Felons Register from Carmarthen manage to provide an historical record and a wealth of information that would otherwise have disappeared with the passing of time.

Henry Westlake was appointed Governor at Carmarthen on 4th July, 1844 after the retirement of John Burnhill. The record preserved in the County Archives at Carmarthen cover the period from 22nd September, 1845-46. The authenticity of the report is preserved in the language of the Governor who although literate has a language of his own. Illiteracy was still wide spread throughout the country and a prisoner who could read and write was considered a remarkable inmate. Because of the effort of Elizabeth Fry schooling and literacy in prison improved. From the recorded evidence of Westlake, even in the Victorian era life in prison was undergoing major changes. No longer filthy rat infested places of deprivation, administered by local magistrates, by 1835 prisons were subject to inspection by the state, and by 1877 total responsibility by the state had been achieved. From this period, visiting magistrates made periodical inspection. Idle prisoners were put to work and the use of white lime was liberally used to improve the décor of the prison walls. These changes are documented in Westlake's record. The tread wheel, introduced as an exercise also had a useful purpose such as grinding corn or, as in the case of Carmarthen, pumping the water from the well.

Extracts from Governor Westlake's Journal

Monday 22nd September, 1845
Captain D. Davies call and I brought John Smith a Prisoner before his worship respecting the order on the back of his commitment that he was to

have the money stoped from his maintenance and I received orders from his worship to deduct what it cost for his maintenance out of his money which was £2-11s-4d. John Smith discharged having served his imprisonment crime a suspected thief.

Tuesday 23rd September
John Smith and James Goulding came to custody committed by G. Davies Mayor Borough Prisoners Crime Rogues and Vagabonds. The former was discharged from this gaol yesterday for similar offence . . . David Lewis came to custody committed by J.E. Saunders Esqr crime Assault the Prisoner his insane for I was obliged to put the straight jacket on him and then to put him in irons and I employed a man to stop in his cell for the night with him. Humphry Polkinghorn Soldier of the 6th Dragoons Discharged he having served his imprisonment and the Remainder of the day employed at the wheel. [From records, John Smith was a vagrant and under the Vagrant Act 1824 'idle and disorderly' persons offending a second time were classified as 'rogues and vagabonds'; on further conviction they became 'incorrigible rogues'.]

Saturday 27th September
Mr Jones assistant Surgeon called and he ordered John Lewis to be put in the Itch ward he having the Itch.

Monday 27th October
. . . I discovered a paper of tobacco thrown over the wall at the back of the wheel which it lodged on the top of the wheel.

Thursday 30th October
John Smith put in the refractory cell upon Bread and Water diet for tearing out a leaf of a hymn book and writing a note to be concealed out of the gaol unknown to me to be sent out by Thomas Morris a discharged prisoner, which it appears that he has some stoleing property at the Blue Boar in Water Street Carmarthen. [On the following day, John Smith again placed in the refractory cell, a room for rebellious prisoners, for destroying the gaol hymnbook]

Monday 10th November
. . . the prisoners attended chapel and school, the wheel was not worked until after dinner in consequence of cleaning and white washing the itch ward . . .

Friday 14th November
James Carter a soldier of the 6th Dragoons came to custody by W. Arwright

19

Capt of the 6ᵗʰ Dragoons crime absent from stable and found drinking and disorderly in a public house sentence 4 days solitary confinement . . .

Saturday 15ᵗʰ November
. . . at 7 o'clock p.m. a corporal of the 6ᵗʰ Dragoons Brought a Drunking Soldier of the same Regiment to this gaol without a commitment for me to keep until he was sober which I informed the corporal that I could not admit him to this gaol but to take him to the police station in the Borough.

Monday 17ᵗʰ November
. . . William Jones a Borough Prisoner sent to bed without is supper for misbehavour on the wheel, the conduct of the prisones at large has been very bad since the Silent system has been put in force and I have to state that it is Impossible to carry out the discipline of the Gaol and House of Correction according to the rules laid down by Sir J. Graham secretary of state, with one Turnkey for his duty is required to be constantly at the entrance of the Gaol.

Wednesday 26ᵗʰ November
. . . David Jones put in Solitary cell for neglecting to work the wheel in his turn and calling George Gilbert a blind eye has he had lost a eye.

Thursday 4ᵗʰ December
. . . William Smith a Borough Prisoner is meat dish taken from him to day for misbehavour in chapel.

Monday 8ᵗʰ December
. . . Mrs Williams wife of Wm. Williams Died this forenoon in the Turnkey Lodge, W. Williams excused from duty.

Thursday 11ᵗʰ December
Prisoners attended chapel and school and the remainder of the day employed at the wheel with the exception of one hour in the afternoon that I stopped the wheel during the time of Mrs Williams going to be buried . . .

Saturday 21ˢᵗ February
. . . I received orders from the Bench of Magistrates . . . not to work the wheel until further orders, but employ the Prisoners picking oakham, and at their different trades, one prisoner picking oakham and two making clogs for shoes and one cleaning the machinery of the pump.

Wednesday 11ᵗʰ March
. . . General orders for the Turnkeys that in future every man and boy, in the

house of correction and the common gaol shall have a number and that the Turnkeys when they have occasion to call on any prisoner or to give him any order address him by his number and not by his name and that no conversation be allowed between the prisoners nor between them and the Turnkeys but that the silent system be adopted as far as practicable . . .

Wednesday 29th July
. . . Having inspected the lock and bolts of the lower Trebanda I found that Thomas Thomas a transport had being trying to make is escape by endeavouring to unscrew screws which fastened the lock of is cell door in making a search I found a piece of old knife in a hole where a brick had been takeing out and a small nail sharpened on a stone which I put him in irons immediately to prevent him from making his escape. [The name Trebanda appears throughout the Governors report and on maps of the time. It is a part of the gaol of the 1800's which was used to house both male and female there is reference to a lower and upper Trebanda, but the significance of the name remains elusive.]

Finally Wednesday 20th September
. . . Charles Davies and David Thomas put in to the refractory cell on bread and water for fighting on the Sabbath day.

Mary Ann Awbery

Even in the 1840's Carmarthen Gaol was not without its regulars. One appears to be Mary Ann Awbery, whose name appears throughout 1845 and 1846. She was considered a nuisance to the community and was frequently in court and subsequently in the gaol. Whilst inside she appears to have refused to conform to the rules of the gaol and on more than one occasion, Governor Westlake refers to her.

In 1846 she entered the prison on 8th July as a Rogue and Vagabond, having only been discharged on 4th July. It was on the following day that Mary Ann Awbery refused to pick her oakham and barricaded her cell by placing her bed against the door. Governor Westlake ordered that the door be forced open and for the remainder of the day two females were placed in her cell to keep watch on her. But when the Governor went to visit her on the 10th she threw her chamber pot and jug at him, just missing his head. For this she was placed in leg irons and then in the refractory [Silent cell]. There she continued to be unruly by refusing to eat her bread and water, which she threw out the window. She remained in solitary confinement for three days.

Mary Ann Awbery was in trouble again on 2nd August for what was described as mutinous conduct and was again placed in leg irons for the day. In the evening, the Governor visited her and offered to remove the irons if she promised to conform. It appears that she refused and the irons were left on over night. The following day the irons were removed and again Mary Ann threw her food and jug at the Governor and the irons were quickly replaced. During the following day she could be heard singing throughout the gaol and the local residents of Spilman Street could even hear the noise. It was on 7th August that Mary Ann was discharged no doubt much to the relief of the staff. But that was not the end. The local police brought her to the gaol on 20th August without a commitment order from the court and the police were told by Governor Westlake to take her to the police station lockup.

Penal Servitude

In the year 1864 saw the introduction of Penal Servitude (punishment and hard labour) and movement towards the centralisation of the Prison system. Penal servitude was the alternative to transportation and more convict prisons were opened, among them Dartmoor and Portland. The convicts sent to these two notorious prisons knew they were in for a hard time – but at least they were not without hope. The new punishment system, while extremely tough, offered incentives to learn a trade and to achieve promotion, privileges and even remission of sentence. By and large the men were engaged on 'public works' from which the community as a whole could benefit – stone quarrying, road building and the construction of quays and breakwaters for dockyards.

There was considerable debate over how to run the state prisons in the future. The main school of thought favoured the separate system in which a prisoner spent his sentence in almost total solitary confinement, working eating and sleeping alone in his cell with only an hour's exercise each day. The theory behind this was that away from the bad influence of other criminals and left alone with his thoughts, a man could be 'softened up' over a period of months and then brainwashed by staff and prison chaplain into leading a better way of life. The loneliness drove some men to madness and suicide, forcing the authorities to modify their ideas so that men would spend only the first two or three months of their sentence in the 'solitary' cell.

On 11th March, 1846, Carmarthen Gaol adopted the silent system under which prisoners were permitted to work and eat together, but were forbidden to speak or look at each other. It was the task of the turnkey to enforce that silence by imposing a discipline based almost entirely upon fear – fear of being put to hard labour on machines, such as the screw and the tread wheel, which would now be classified as instruments of torture. Even the females at the gaol were subjected to the silent system and so great was the fear of solitary confinement that all abided to the rule.

The Felons' Register

Every picture tells a story. This is certainly true of the many images captured on film and recorded for posterity by the Governor of Carmarthen Gaol, George Stephens (appointed 4th September, 1847). A keen amateur photographer he was not the first to capture the faces of prisoners, but he was quick to see that with a photograph identification prisoners found it difficult to change identities at a time when aliases were in frequent use. Many prisoners tried to sabotage his efforts by pulling faces or puffing up their cheeks. With the variety of crime and punishment in the county together with the frequency that some entered the gaol, it was an understandable ploy.

The modern and violent crime of today was far from being unknown in rural Carmarthenshire. Violent crime is considered by some to be the scourge of modern days, yet it also had its place in Victoria's reign and that the human beings inhumanity to his fellow being is no modern phenomenon. The crimes of the 1800's were just as cold and calculated, as the felon's register bears out. Some of the entries are amusing as well as being shocking for the reader.

Thomas Jones, 10th January, 1844 transported for 10 years. His crime was that of house burglary. Only nine days later Francis Davis 17 years old received 12 months hard labour. The following day on 20th January, John Thomas, a 61 year old, married with two children was transported for 10 years, for causing a riot and robbery. On the same day David Thomas, age 37 was transported for 20 years for the same offence. Thomas Thomas age 34 and Thomas Powell age 23 each received a sentence of 10 years transportation for riot and robbery. All four men were tried by Sir William Henry Maule.

John Evans, 8th June, 1844 at the age of 21 had spent time at the Swansea House of Correction. Almost as soon as he had been released, he was again in trouble this time in Carmarthen Town. He was accused of stealing *'women's apparel'*. For this he was sentenced to nine months at Carmarthen Gaol.

William Curwood, 1847 accused of 'carnally knowing and abusing a child of 3½'. The case was dismissed but it shows that child abuse was not unknown before the *'permissive society'* and the pitiful stories we hear today of acts committed on children.

Anne Davies, 30th June, 1848 had been remanded in custody on a felony charge, considered in its day to be very serious. Her offence was *'Unlawfully Milking a Cow'*. However, she was acquitted.

Prisoner 233 Daniel Jones, 10th February, 1847 was committed to gaol accused of attempting to commit suicide, *Felo de se* [self-murderer, or self-harm], this was a crime and the punishment was imprisonment. **John Walters**, prison number 325 was transported for 10 years for stealing 14 lambs from Penallt Farm, Kidwelly.

James Watkins, prisoner 378, 17th August, 1851 was committed accused of bestiality, a common rural offence of the day. When John Davies in 1856 entered the gaol it was for the sixth occasion, his first committal was at the age of 10. The case of Elizabeth Ready age 12 and Ellen Dowd aged 11. Both children were charged with stealing a workbox and were sentenced to one month's hard labour. Neither girl had been in custody before, but Ellen's mother had been in gaol for larceny. The child was no doubt following the parent's example; something that is still not uncommon in our modern gaols.

Richard Vivian in 1860 was a 26-year-old clerk in Llanelli; he received 7 days hard labour for stealing cricket balls. Yet two years later Hiram Lane, prison number 926, a 10-year-old boy labourer was committed on 30th July, 1862 for stealing bread and cheese. A case of the theft of food was considered more serious than the theft of cricket balls, and Hiram was sentenced to 14 days and then sent to 'Howdref Ganol Reformatory' near Neath for 5 years. In 1864 14-year-old John Evans and 13-year-old Daniel McCarthy, followed Hiram to the Reformatory for 'attempting to steal strawberries'. They both received 14 days in Carmarthen Gaol and then three years at Neath Reformatory School.

George Adams died in prison on 29th July, 1864 from a heart attack, four days after his admission. He had been sent to prison for stealing a donkey. The governor had made an entry in the record that Adams's appearance was 'fresh and good looking'. No doubt, news of his death, after just four days in custody must have been like a bolt of lightning to the governor.

In 1865 the felons register also records what must be the original Great Train Robbery, when George Bryant and Isaac Cromley, an engine driver and fireman on the South Wales Railway, committed the crime of stealing cider and peppermint that their train was carrying. These early Great

Train Robbers received one month's hard labour for their crime.

The register records young and old, many transported for what today are considered minor offences. One punishment that has to serve as a deterrent for our modern vandals has to be that of ten-year-old David Jones who on 11th November, 1869 was found guilty of placing a stone on the track of the South Wales Railway. For this he received one month's hard labour at Carmarthen Gaol. As if that alone was not enough, he was then whipped with 15 straps of the birch.

The Pillory
The last man put in the Pillory at Carmarthen

The wooden frame with holes for the head and arms, in which the wrongdoer was mocked in public stood in Carmarthen for many years. Thomas Evans, or Tomos Glyn Cothi, the noted Unitarian preacher, was the last man to use it around 1813. Like all true prophets, he was in advance of his time. He was a man who was not afraid to speak out and dared to rebel against the existing order of the day and strike out for the principle of freedom and equality among his fellow man. Thomas Evans was made of sterner stuff than most of his contemporaries; he would speak out for the French Revolution and the great French wars and for the rights of the poor in the courts of the land. He was suspected of Jacobinism. Tomos's views were closely scrutinised and it was in 1802 that he was sent to gaol for two years and placed in the pillory for singing in public 'The Hymn to Liberty', from an adaptation of 'The Marseillaise Hymn'. He insisted on purchasing a new waistcoat and overcoat for the occasion. His daughter stood at his side while he was at the pillory and when one woman in the crowd threw a rotten egg at his head the crowd turned on the woman. Whatever the authorities thought of his outspokenness Tomos Glyn Cothi had found sympathetic ears among the people of Carmarthen.

When he was in gaol, he is noted to have written an English Welsh dictionary, which was published in 1817. After his time in gaol, he went to live in Aberdare and died as the minister of Hen Dy-Cwrdd on 29th January 1833, age 68.

As can be seen with the Penal Code it was extreme in its severity, with public hangings, and transportation for what today would be considered trivial offences. The public called for a change in the law. It has already been mentioned, that in 1832, there were 120 offences for which the death sentence was applied. It was not until Robert Peel entered parliament as

Home Secretary (1822-1827 and again from 1828-1830), that a complete reform of the penal system and the abolition of over a hundred crimes that the death penalty was called for. The severity of the Penal Code, actually encouraged more serious crime. This is born out from the saying:

I might as well be hanged for a sheep as a lamb.

Prisons were still considered to be dens of iniquity even after the reforms of Robert Peel. Improvement were slow, but without the pioneering work of people like Howard, Fry and Peel reform would have been much slower. Many of our modern prison have been built on the suggestions of these early pioneers.

Chapter 3

Carmarthen a Lawless town

Sir Robert Peel, son of a rich cotton manufacturer, entered Parliament in 1809. It was in his term as Home Secretary (1822-27, 1828-30) that he introduced the first police force in London, known as Peelers or Bobbies. As can be imagined, they were not a popular force. Many considered them an infringement on English social and political life and the police were often jeered as they went about their business.

It was during the Parliamentary election riots of 1831 at Carmarthen when the then Chief Constable found that he could not control the mobs violently rioting in the town with his meagre force of four watchmen. The watchmen, it was said had been drawn from the same lower orders as the rioting mob and were easily led astray and often joined in the affray. Law and order was by now nonexistent and after a plea to London, the Home Secretary deployed six of Robert Peel's Bobbies to Carmarthen. They arrived on 20th August, 1831 and were supported by a troop of the 14th Dragoons and the 98th regiment at Llandeilo. With a large number of local special constables employed, several were seriously injured before some semblance of law and order was obtained.

William Spurrell 1813-1889

William Spurrell was the third son of Richard Spurrell, Clerk of the Carmarthen Justices. Educated in the local Queen Elizabeth Grammar School, at the age of 16 he became apprentice to a local printer in Carmarthen. After five years, he left for London and became involved in the production of the first editions of Dickens' Pickwick Papers and Nicholas Nickelby. On his return to Carmarthen in 1839, he opened his own printing firm that flourished for nearly one hundred years in Carmarthen.

Carmarthen is indebted to him as it is from his publication of 1879, 'Carmarthen and its Neighbourhood' that the town has retained a true recording of its colourful past. From Spurrell's book, visitors can find places of interest both new and old.

From Spurrell's work, we have an account of conditions in and around Carmarthen from AD 52 to 1879. It was during this later period that many public hangings took place. Carmarthen had established itself as a town where major crime was almost unknown but the poor of the town indulged in theft, if only to survive. As a result, the penalties for these crimes were high; hard labour, transportation or hanging. Spurrell wrote much about the past but it is in his presentation of the hangings in and around Carmarthen that his accounts have proved invaluable to historians.

Spurrell published accounts of one of the old inhabitants of the town. Many of these stories would have gone unrecorded had it not been for Spurell's collective work. No dates can be attributed to these early events, as memory often forgets the date, just recounting the occasion.

The old man recalled that a Welsh Bard had once been locked in the town pillory on four occasions. His crime was 'Doing something against the government'. One interesting occasion related was when an old man was due to hang at Pensarn for stealing a mare. It appears that no one in the town would stand as executioner. A prisoner in the gaol sentenced to 14 years transportation, volunteered to do the deed on one condition that he received a lesser sentence. The old man went to the gallows at Pensarn and the prisoner, come executioner, had his wish, he was transported for seven years and not the fourteen. As a final twist, the gallows was stolen during the night after the execution and the timber it is said was used to make a bed.

Spurrell's book also recounts the removal of the old gate at each end of King Street, and the Dark Gate, and the poor debtors letting their bags down on cord, soliciting aid in their accustomed phrase, 'remember the poor debtors'. The old inhabitant describes an office over this gate with thirteen steps leading up, and the unruly children of the time threatened with being sent to the thirteen steps, for whatever fate should await them up there. Finally, the old inhabitant recounted French prisoners in the gaol, following the French invasion at Fishguard in 1797 and the curiosity of the people of Carmarthen at the sight and strange conversations from these foreigners.

It was in the Market place on 26th February, 1555 that it is recorded that *David Grifeith Leyson, High Sherife of Carmarthenshire personally handed over the custody of Bishop Ferrar, in St Peter's Church, to Morgan his successor, who committed him to the keeping of Owen Jones.*

On 30th March, being *the Saturday next before Passion Sunday. 'This yeare Bishopp Fferrar the martyr was burnt in the market place where the conduit Is'. David Grifeith Leyson, LL.D. of Carmarthen Priory, Principle of St Edward's Hall Oxford, a justice of the peace, and high sherife for Carmarthenshire, who had turned Papist in Queen Mary's reign, 'would not suffer him to speak at the stake. Leyson died soon after, and when he would have spoken, could not.' Richard Jones (or Johnes), of Cwmgwilli, son of Sir Thomas Jones, of Abermarlais, first M.P. for Pembrokeshire, called to console Bishop Ferrar under sentence.*

It is in the year 1568 that the first executions are mentioned by Spurrell. The first was that of David William Parry, a High Sheriff and Bishop Ferrar's brother's eldest son, he and Sir Gelly Meyrick and others were considered traitors to Queen Elizabeth 1 and were duly hanged. In 1633 Father Arthur, an Irishman, believed to be a Jesuit, was hung drawn and quartered for conspiring the Kings death; his offence was to curse the King.

In 1665 Nicholas Williams, Rhydodyn, sheriff,

In his sherifeship a woman, viz., gwraig Wil Goch, was burnt, and one of her daughters and a servant man hanged for killing her husband, and another daughter condemned, and after a long confinement was discharged.

On 22nd May, 1739, a man by the name of Edwards, from the village of Llandefeilog, was hanged at Pensarn. His crime was pilfering. On the following day 23rd May Elinor Williams, alias Hadley, a servant at Job's Well, was hanged on the common below the Royal Oak Gate, for the murder of her child. Buried near the town railway station her body is said to have been gibbeted before burial. On the same day, two lads were executed for stealing cider from Mr Evan Thomas Landlord of the Greyhound Inn Carmarthen.

It was in the year 1742 that a girl of eight was tried at Carmarthen Assizes. She had been charged with the murder of her brother and sister, six and four respectively. It would appear that the children were frightened by the stories going around about the cruelty inflicted by the Spaniards and the expected Spanish invasion. During the night, a violent thunderstorm erupted and the children thought that it was the invading Spaniards. The young children begged their sister to kill them. She carried out the murders with a blade used to cut hedging. She then tried to use the blade on herself. It is on record that this young child was acquitted at her trial.

In 1745, Robin Lewis Richard of Abergwili, was hanged for the murder of William Owen of Carmarthen. Two years later in 1747 a Captain Owens, a smuggler of note hanged for the murder of a dance instructor. The year 1750 records the execution of Joseph Jenkins, *'a noted swearer was committed to the town gaol for the murder of his wife'*. Having been convicted he was hanged on the common near the Royal Oak Gate. St Peter's Register records the murder as *'1750 December 11th'*.

It was on 28th March, 1770 that nine prisoners were condemned to death at Hereford, before Mr Justice Yates and Baron Perrott, for the murder of William Powell, of Glanareth, Llangadock, in his parlour, on the 8th January. On the 22nd March, all nine men had been removed from Carmarthen Gaol and taken to Hereford by *Habeas Corpus*. Of the nine who had been tried, William Spiggott, alias Spickett, William Morris, David Morris, David Morgan, alias Lacey, William Walter Evan, Charles David Morgan, and David Llewellyn, of Llandovery, were found guilty and were all hanged at Hereford on 30th March. William Spiggott and William Walter Evan later hanged in chains. William Thomas, alias Blink John Spiggott and William Charles were acquitted, but William Thomas returned to live in Carmarthen and was hanged at Pensarn for horse stealing. Walter Evan had turned King's evidence, but was later hanged for further crimes

A trail of footprints and spots of blood in the snow were traced to Charles David Morgan; and it was he who accused several of his accomplices. The evidence was given in Welsh, and it was claimed that William Williams was the instigator and ringleader of the gang of assassins. He was never brought before the court as he had fled the country and was living in France.

William Powell had been murdered because William Williams wanted to marry Powell's wife. Of the twenty wounds inflicted on Powell, it was proved by the prosecution that any one of eight would have caused death. At his funeral, his coffin covered with a scarlet cloth to show that he had been murdered. From records, it was proved that William Powell's wife had planned her husband's murder. The wife of William Williams was also aware that her husband was trying to murder her. On one occasion he had attempted to hang her and on another he had put white powder into her tea, and it was only that her child had said that Williams had put some sugar from his pocket into the cup that saved her life. The tea was later given to the family dog and some days later, it died.

As to what became of Williams in France, he was taken prisoner by a French privateer, but escaped and fled to St Omer were he became a schoolteacher. However, he drowned when he took a party of schoolchildren on a cruise. In his papers at Boulogne, they found a pocket book with a blood spot and an entry on the page of 8th January, 1770 read *'My finger bled to-day how singular'*. The tale continues with the story of the man who had interpreted at the court proceedings was fired at as he made his way home, by a man disguised in an ass's skin, who had leapt over the hedge. No record appears to mention of any conviction for this offence.

The year 1788 was a busy one for the executioner at Pensarn with several executions. One of these was Will Mani, for murdering a woman on Pembrey Mountain. The cuff from his coat was found in his victim's hand and it was this cuff that was identified by a tailor and it convicted Mani. He hanged and later gibbeted on the mountain at Pensarn. Gutto (Grifeith) Rowley was charged with the murder of a tithe collector. Rowley escaped to Bristol where he worked in a sugar warehouse for several years. It was only when he attempted to rob a pig drover from Llanddarog, on Bristol Bridge that he was recognised and arrested. Some ten years later his son was executed for being involved in the robbery of his aunt and her attempted murder.

In 1789, John Nash began to construct the new County Gaol. With its completion in 1792 all the prisoners were transferred from the town gaol to the new County Gaol, which stood on the gate between King Street and Market Street (Nott Square).

The next execution to take place was that of Sioni'r Cornell, a shoemaker, who in 1797 murdered his father at Llanfihangel, Abercowin. He was hanged at Pensarn. On 4th August, 1802 records show that a person stood in the pillory.

In 1810, the Borough Gaol was completed and on 27th August, all the town prisoners were transferred to the new lock up. At the County Gaol in June 1814, a dungeon had been discovered deep under ground it was described as having a stout wooded pillar in the middle of the room. It was assumed at the time that the condemned criminals were fastened to this pillar prior to execution.

It was on 30th March, 1825, that William Butterton was appointed Governor of the County Gaol in place of Benjamin Waugh who had died. However, he also died that year and a new Governor had to be appointed. This was John Burnhill.

Three men were arrested on 2nd November, 1834 for burglary of a warehouse, and sentenced to transportation to the colonies. Whilst awaiting transportation they attempted to escape from Carmarthen Gaol. The attempt failed and they were promptly despatched to the colonies.

The 4th July, 1844 saw the appointment of Henry Westlake as Governor of the County Gaol on the retirement of John Burnhill. His appointment lasted until 1847 when George Stevens replaced him. Stevens continued as Governor until his retirement on 17th October, 1878 and was replaced by Owen Thomas. However, before Stevens retired he witnessed the change over when the County Gaol came under the authority of the State on 1st April, 1878.

The 4th January, 1866 was the date when two prisoners, Owen Pritchard (29) and John Reid (16) escaped from Carmarthen Gaol. They used a piece of wood to make a hole into each other's cell and then broke into a chimney flue to gain access to the prison yard. Then with their bed sheets and a weighted pillowcase they scaled the prison wall. Pritchard was arrested the following day, having been chased by a policeman. In the words of Spurrell, *'He was a desperate character; and when taken was bare footed, and armed with a pointed hedge-stake, to which he made significant reference; two sharp raps on the head showed him that his observations were duly appreciated'.*

In 1832, a noted character from Pembrokeshire drove a cart of smuggled spirits through the town, and was pursued by a body of excise men, who had lain in ambush near the Royal Oak Gate. Putting his horse into a gallop, he outdistanced his pursuers, escaped with his cart over the bridge, and deposited his load in safety near Llanarthney. He later drowned near Pembroke, having run into the water in endeavouring to escape from the officers of a revenue cutter who were trying to arrest him. He used to keep casks of spirit under a stone in the floor of his pigsty. On one occasion, not having time to put them in the usual place of concealment, customs officers visited him, he was able to keep the customs officers at bay with a red-hot poker, while his son stove in the casks, and poured the spirit down the drain.

And they blessed Rebekah and said to her
Thou art our sister
Be thou the mother of thousands of millions,
And let thy seed possess the gate of those which hate them.
Genesis 24.60

The Rebecca Riots 1843

It was in 1843 that the Rebecca riots broke out. They were rioting against the charges at the tollgates on the public roads, and against the increase in tithe charges. The rioters adopted the verse from Genesis as their motto. Using the words of the Bible, many of the rioters disguised themselves as women and rode on horseback; each band was under a leader known only as 'Rebecca', the followers known as the daughters of Rebecca. They destroyed not only the gates but also the tollhouses. The raids were carried out in the dead of night, usually without injury to the toll keepers, but as time went on injuries and some fatal injuries did occur.

In the early days of the riots, many people attempted to pass through the gates without paying and were duly fined by the magistrate. When the local constables tried to collect the fine, they refused to pay and the constables returned empty handed. On one-occasion, thirty pensioners were sworn in to assist the constables with the execution of the warrants, and were employed to collect the fine of a man called Harries of Talog. They seized goods from his house and set about returning to Carmarthen with the goods. A short distance from Carmarthen they were surrounded by about 400 Rebeccaites and were forced to march to the home of Captain Davies. At Trawsmawr, it was he who had signed the warrants. The pensioners were ordered to demolish the walls around Trawsmawr and at the end of the day, they returned to Carmarthen empty handed. During the night of 10th June, the rioters set about destroying the plantations at Trawsmawr.

During the month of June various secret meetings took place and on 14th June it was decided that a march on Carmarthen was called for. Rich and poor were all required to attend or have their houses and barns burnt down, and on 19th June, 1843, at eleven o'clock, people met at the Plough and Harrow, Bwlch Newydd. Some 2000 Rebeccaites were expected to march on Carmarthen, but on the day, 3000 were believed to have attended. They arrived about noon, marching four or five abreast. The procession reached from the gaol and went on through Spilman Street, Church Street, and St Peter's Street to the King Street end of Conduit Lane. No violence was expected on the day, as the protest was to be peaceful but as the 'Town roughs' met the marchers they led them to the workhouse and trouble ensured. The authorities became concerned, as next door to the workhouse was a brewery. If the rioters turned their attention to this the contents could easily fuel the riot. A company of Dragoons had been expected early in the morning. They were long overdue, and search parties had been sent out to look for them. They were found some distance away and escorted to Carmarthen at full gallop arriving just in time to save the workhouse, and the brewery. It appeared that locals in the area of Pontardullais had misdirected them

In the words of William Spurrell:

They were met by T.C. Morris Esq., Mayor, who rode on with their officer. Sweeping through Red Street and Barn Row, they charged at a gallop up the hill, their armour glistening in the sun. Just at this instant the work of destruction had begun, the beds being thrown out through windows. It was amusing to witness the consternation the arrival of the soldiers occasioned. The country people fled in every direction, like ants when an ant hill is disturbed; fleeing they new not whither, none seeming to look back. A good number were taken within the workhouse walls; many of them being curious spectators of what was going on.

This was not the end of the rioting. During the following months many tollgates and tollhouses around the area were destroyed and many were injured. On 9th September at midnight, a gang set the house on fire, and shot Sarah Williams, a seventy five year old toll collector at the Hendy Gate Llanedi.

The 11th October saw the arrival of fifty London 'Bobbies' who assisted the military to be followed by another twenty London police officers. Still the riots continued.

It was during this period that Carmarthen Gaol played a major role in detaining the rioters. Many of the ringleaders were imprisoned in the gaol and from 1st January, 1844 special court sessions were held to try the ringleaders. Sentencing varied from life in prison to transportation to the colonies for periods ranging from 10 to 20 years or even life.

Two of the most notorious leaders were Sioni Scybor Fawr and Dai y Cantwr. Sioni described as a real ruffian, was convicted of some of the most heinous crimes during the riots, and for his part received a sentence of transportation for life.

Dai was described as an entirely different man and deserved the pity generally extended to him. He received a sentence of twenty years transportation. While in prison he wrote a lament, which has been translated from, Welsh to English:

'I am the spectacle to the world
I have lost the reputation that I might have obtained
Severe is the stroke, the sad buffet
To the reach of which I am brought
In my youth adversity came
Instead of liberty, long captivity
Has been added to my grief
I am an exile at the beginning of my course
I shall be sent from my country

From my fathers house, notwithstanding tender bringing up
To the midst of black hordes
Over the sea, from my fair confines
Oh what distress (literally bad weather) has overtaken me!
Long banishment, this will drive me bound
For twenty years
Hard is the measure, long affliction.'

Dai y Cantwr, 1844

It was not until 1844 that the riots were finally suppressed and this was followed with an inquiry into their cause. It resulted in the passing of the South Wales Turnpike Act.

Whitehall
June 21, 1845

Gentlemen,
I am commanded by the Queen to express her desire to contribute the sum of two hundred guineas towards the erection of a monument in honour of the late Sir William Nott. Her Majesty sends this contribution as a mark of her memory of that gallant officer, and of her high sense of the distinguished Services which he rendered to his Country.

I have the honour to be
Gentlemen
Your obedient Servant
Robert Peel

Sir William Nott
Born January 20th 1782, died January 1st 1845

A son of Carmarthen returned to Carmarthen in 1844 following a distinguished career in India during the 1800s. At the close of his career, he retrieved the military character of his nation in central Asia by repelling the attempts of the Afghans to recapture Candahar between 1841 and 1843. It was after the destruction of the Afghan army at Cabool and with a force of some five and six thousand men, he advanced on Ghusnee on 7th August 1842. He defeated the Afghan army a force said to be twenty thousand strong, and set about destroying the fortifications and returned to the safe boundaries of

Western Provinces of Upper India with his victorious army.

With his death, Carmarthen lost a distinguished son. He received a state funeral with some 22 carriages and escorted by soldiers of the 41st and 13th regiments and a monument was erected in his honour.

Chapter 4

The Sentence of Death

That you, be taken to the place from whence you came and from thence be drawn on a hurdle to the place of execution, where you shall be hanged by the neck, not till you are dead; that you be taken down, while yet alive, and your bowels taken out and burnt before your face-that your head be then cut off, and your body cut in quarters, to be at the King's disposal. And God Almighty have mercy on your soul.

This was the sentence read out to the condemned up until the 1820's, clearly explaining to the victim what fate awaited him. It had been the sentence of the court for over five hundred years, first used in the reign of Edward lll (1327-1377) in the 14th century. A form was known to exist as early as 1283, when Dafydd, the last native Prince of Wales, was executed in Shrewsbury. This was during the reign of Edward I (1272-1307) when in 1283 Edward I subjugated the whole of Wales following the Welsh revolt of 1282 when Llywelyn ap Gruffydd was killed followed with the execution of his brother Dafydd.

By the 1820s reforms were afoot dissection of the body after the execution was discontinued the wording on passing sentence of death to the accused was amended to the following:

The sentence of the court upon you is, that you be taken from this place to a lawful prison and thence to a place of execution and that you be hanged by the neck until you are dead; and that your body be afterwards buried within the precincts of the prison in which you shall be confined before your execution. And may the Lord have mercy on your soul.
Amen

'The ugliest of trades have their moments of pleasure. Now, if I were a grave-digger, or even a hangman, there are some people I could work for with a great deal of enjoyments'.

Douglas Jerrold
1803-1857

Hangman and Executioner

To be able to expose the myth of the office of executioner, we must first look at the history of the hangman. Many crowded to view this public spectacle, with its clumsiness and numerous botched executions. With head and limbs torn from the body, the crowds cried out for more and more. To view the dissected body after the execution was considered to be the climax of the day's festivities.

From the classes of nobility they were not. Hangmen came from all lifestyles. We hear of one at Carmarthen who volunteered to do the job on condition that his 14-year sentence of deportation was reduced. Many hangmen were assaulted and many were no better than the criminals they had come to execute. Many a hangman ended his days on the gallows himself. They were considered the lowest of the low. The executioner is at once the most feared and hated and to see the hangman at the cell door saying 'Come with me' or 'It's time', knowing you are walking to your death must be our most feared nightmare. But at the end of the day they were only an extension of the court and if no one condemns the 'Hanging Judge' then who are we to shun the 'Tool' who carries out the sentence of the court.

Many early hangmen tried to hide their identities and yet in latter days they openly displayed their trade with calling cards and fine letterheads. For many centuries, all who encountered them shunned them. Hangmen were portrayed in travelling Punch and Judy shows. In fairs and market places, Mr Punch would murder his wife and then outwit the hangman to the delight of the watching crowd.

Our every day-spoken language has been enlarged with many phrases from the past centuries and we take them for granted without a single thought of their origins. Take the name Derrick. He was a hangman from the early seventeenth century whose name later came to describe a device for hoisting heavy objects or a crane.

Then, every service man will know the phrase 'Toe the line'. This originated from the condemned having to cooperate with his executioner by standing on a line while the hangman left the platform to make final adjustments before he sent the poor soul into eternity. Even the thought that ladders are unlucky comes from the days of executions, when the condemned were made to climb a ladder to the gallows. In this modern day prison staff use the words 'To shoot the Bolt' referring to the lock on the cell door when entering a cell you shoot the bolt to prevent being locked in. The origin of this term comes from the executioner pushing the lever to open the trap.

> *All ye that in the condemned hold doth lie,*
> *Prepare ye, for tomorrow you shall die.*
> *Watch and pray, the hour is drawing near.*
> *That you before the Almighty must appear;*
> *Examine well yourselves, in time repent,*
> *That you may not to eternal flames be sent;*
> *And when St Sepulchre's Bell in the morning tolls,*
> *The Lord above have mercy on your souls.*

The Bellman
St Sepulchre's Church
Tyburn London 1612

William Calcraft

In the early days, hangmen employed a short drop, which in effect strangled the man and would have him struggling on the end of the rope for several minutes, much to the delight of the watching crowds. They would flock in their thousands from near and far to witness to the event. One of the most prolific of these early hangmen was William Calcraft whose name has gone down in the annals of hangmen as being one of the most callous of all. He played to the crowds turning the day into a **'Hangman's Holiday'**. Many women climbed onto the gallows after the event to have the hand of the executed placed on them and in so doing, it was considered that this would cure various blemishes like warts and wens and other ailments.

Calcraft was not a man of science or of an inquiring mind. Born near Chelmsford in 1800, he went to London to seek his fortune. It was at a public hanging that Calcraft began to show an interest in the profession. Unlike his predecessors, he had not come from a criminal background. Only in later years did he cross swords with the law and then only for minor offences. He attended executions gaily dressed often with a flower in his button unlike many who would attend in black. He said, *'I must keep my client in good spirits. Besides, I'm not a parson or an undertaker'.*

Calcraft was known as a bungler who would strangle the condemned to death. A year before his retirement in 1868 a reporter left an eyewitness account:

The execution of James O'Connor 1867

The robed priest walked directly in front of the condemned, a bound figure. Next hobbled an aged, palsied, trembling man, Calcraft, the official executioner. At the foot of the fatal tree, Father Bonte offered O'Connor a crucifix to kiss, which he did with evident devotion. I shuddered as Calcraft placed the rope round the victim's throat and drew it tight. The white robed priest – last friend of the dying man on earth, read on. A crash! A thud! The end has come! No; the rope flies loosely in the air! What has happened? With a vault Father Bonte sprang into the pit, his priestly vestments flying in the wind I followed him. Propped up against the wooden partition lay O'Connor the broken rope around his neck, and the white cap over his eyes. Seizing my arm with his pinioned hands he exclaimed: 'I stood it bravely, didn't I? You will let me off now, won't you? Let me off do!' Think of the horror of that appeal! 'You will let me off, won't you?' And there was no power to do so. 'There to be hanged by the neck until you are dead,' was the dread sentence, and the law must be obeyed. The half hanged man was supported by warders and taken behind the scaffold, while the other officials hurriedly procured a new rope, and then again he was placed in position. Calcraft pulled the lever, the drop fell, and James O'Connor was dead.

unknown

It was decided that drastic measures were needed to improve on the quick disposal of the countries worst criminals. Along came William Marwood who described Calcraft as follows:

Ah, Calcraft came from a family of slow worms. He chocked his prisoners to death. He throttled them, but I executed them.

Calcraft continued until his retirement claiming that a long painful death on the gallows was what the *Capital Punishment* called for. He proclaimed, *'The hangman was not in the market for reform. Instant death could not improve on lingering death as a deterrent to others who had thoughts about murder of ones own human beings'.*

When Calcraft retired in 1868 it was proclaimed that the day of the hangman was over. In future there were executioners.

William Marwood

I'd sooner be a serpent stung
Or hugg'd by a grizzly bear,
Or crush'd by one of Pickford's vans,
Or blown into the air;
I'd sooner be by Marwood Hung
Than have the least connection
With deceitful Emma Hay.

Music Hall Ballard

William Marwood looked at the methods used in execution and looked at them in a more scientific way. He changed Calcraft's slow suffocation to a long calculated drop and quick death. He developed a drop that would break the vertebrae in the neck and in so doing result in a loss of sensation to the condemned and a painless death. He practised his method in a backroom at his workshop and in the end he produced a table which others used to calculate the length of the rope to produce the correct drop.

James Berry

My brother, sit and think,
While yet on earth some hours are left to thee,
Kneel to thy God, who does not from thee shrink,
And lay thy sins on Christ, who died for thee.
James Berry

A non-conformist lay preacher, Berry recited the above words to the victim on the way to the gallows. Much to the dissatisfaction of the waiting dignitaries, he often slowed the proceeding so that he could talk to the victim and thus obtained many a confession. Berry slept better after the execution if a confession of guilt was obtained. He felt that as he was the last human being with them the victim, he formed a special bond, he often said:

They don't tell lies to the hangman.

Berry disliked the term *'Hangman'* and much preferred the word

'*Executioner*'. This he believed carried a more dignified terminology for the public duty he performed. To this end he had floral calling cards produced showing his address, name and occupation.

Berry first appeared at Carmarthen for the execution of David Rees in 1888. Following in the footsteps of Marwood, he was well versed in the long drop method and the authorities were quick to use his skills. He improved on the table of execution. A shoe salesman from Bradford, he was considered the perfect replacement.

Despite his habit of slowing the precession to obtain a confession, it never seemed to worry him about the guilt or innocence of the victim. It was enough to know that they had been found guilty. He was not the judge of innocence or guilt. That was for the court of the land to decide, he was just the tool with which to carry out the sentence of the court. With his improvements, he claimed that he could get the job done, from cell to execution in three minutes. He once made the following statement:

I enter the cell punctually at three minutes to eight. When we enter the condemned cell the Chaplain is already there, and he has been for some time. The attendants who watch through the convict's last night on earth are also present. At my appearance the convict takes leave of his attendants to whom he generally gives some small token or keepsake, and I at once proceed to pinion his arms. As soon as the pinioning is done a procession is formed.

On the way from the cell to the scaffold the Chaplain reads the service for the burial of the dead, and as the procession moves, I place the white cap upon the head of the convict. Just as we reach the scaffold I pull the cap over his eyes. Then I place the convict under the beam, pinion his legs just below the knees, adjust the rope, pull the bolt and the trap falls. Death is instantaneous.

James Berry
1852-1913

James Billington

'Behold the Lord High Executioner
A personage of noble rank and title
A dignified and potent officer,
Whose functions are particularly vital!
To the Lord High Executioner'

W S Gilbert

James Billington, a native of Bolton replaced Berry as Chief Executioner. On leaving school he worked in the local mill and at night helped his father in the family barbershop later, he went to work in the pit, before taking over the family business A keen sportsman, and despite his height of 5ft 4ins he was described as a plucky and courageous man. He had a hatred for reporters and would always try to alter his appearance to outwit the press who followed him from railway station to prison and back hoping for snippets for their next editions. Those who were brave enough to follow him into his shop pretending to be customers would leave with half a shave. No doubt they were lucky, to get away with that, for as they plagued him with questions with a sharp razor at their throat on many an occasion he was understandably tempted to just slit their throats and in so doing reduce the number of inquisitive reporters.

James Billington only appeared twice at Carmarthen. The year was 1894, and the occasions were the execution of George Thomas in the February and Thomas Richards in November. This was the last time that the Death Bell rang and the black flag was flown in Carmarthen. No further executions took place and the prison closed in 1922. However, executions continued at Swansea Prison up until 1958.

The Black Flag

The flying of the black flag, which measured 8 x 4, hoisted over the gaol gate was to signal to the waiting crowd that the execution had taken place. The other tradition of ringing the prison bell also came to an end a few years later when in another prison a quadruple execution was about to take place and it was thought by the authorities that the sound of the bell would prove to be too stressful for the waiting to be hung. The only outward sign that an execution had taken place after that was the notice posted on the prison gate. However, even this practice stopped in 1957, long after Carmarthen had closed its gate for all time.

Chapter 5

Executions

Many of the earlier executions were recorded in William Spurrells book, but it was with the advent of the weekly newspaper that more detailed accounts were recorded. They are a true record of the feelings of the time.

A letter dated 1752 from Grifeith Philipps of Cwmgwili to his son George in London says:

> *there are this day to be hang'd at Carmarthen two men for house breaking, which I suppose will draw al ye country peoples together, it being a very uncommon thing here to get em hang'd by pairs.*

Another letter dated 1788, from Richard Jones, Carmarthen, to John Philipps, M.P. stated:

> *we had three persons condemned, two for horse stealing and one for stealing goods and breaking into a house in the day time; this last was the hangman in the gaol, a person not 20 years of age, who had been tried at our bar three times; not half an hour after he received sentence he hung himself in the gaol.*

A large number of executions are recorded as having taken place at Carmarthen:

Edward Higgins   **Executed 7th November, 1767**

It was in the year of 1767 on 11th September, that the whole of the County became excited over the reported escapades of the notorious Edward Higgins described, as a housebreaker and burglar.

The Carmarthen County Hall was crowded on the morning 11th September, 1767, when Edward Higgins stood in the dock awaiting trial for the burglary of Lady Maud and Madam Bevan's residence at

44

Laugharne. The trial lasted all-day and late into the evening and in the end, the jury found Higgins guilty. Due to the lateness of the hour, the crowd had to wait until the following day for the judge to pass sentence. Therefore, it was early on the morning of the 12th September, 1767 that the judge entered the crowded courtroom, placed the black cap on his head, and passed the sentence of death on Edward Higgins.

Edward Higgins, aged 42, born in 1725, was described as a Highwayman. However, his luck had run out at Laugharne when he had been seen acting suspiciously by the local constable and had tried to evade arrest. It was only with the intervention of Mr Rowe who was out exercising his dog and saw the constable struggling with Higgins on the floor, that the highwayman was overpowered and arrested. Throughout his trial, Higgins denied that he had committed any crime but the evidence was to prove otherwise. When he was searched part of a key was found in his pocket, and this matched a fragment of key found in the lock of the trunk of Lady Maud's. Also an Almanac missing from the same trunk was found in his possession. It was not until Higgins climbed the scaffold and handed the Under Sheriff a letter that the truth about this highwayman finally come out.

One of Higgins' earlier court appearances was around 1752 at Worcester for sheep stealing, but on this occasion he received an acquittal of the offence. On another occasion, he appeared in court in 1754 for house breaking and, having been found guilty on two indictments, was transported to Maryland for seven years. At Boston, he escaped custody, broke into a merchant's house, and stole money to pay for his return passage to England. Within three months of leaving England, he was back. Soon after his return to England, he married into a respectable family and moved to Knutsford in Cheshire. There he befriended the gentry of Knutsford. He owned a pack of hounds and hunters and frequently joined in with the local hunts and other field sports of the gentry in the neighbourhood; he would hunt with them in the morning, dine with them in the afternoon, and raid their homes at night. There he set about carrying on with the pretence of living a respectable life. He would leave home for weeks on end with the pretence of collecting rent from houses he owned throughout the country; his wife at the time was unaware of his true vocation in life.

One of his more daring burglaries took place in Chester on Friday morning of Christmas week. There had been a ball, which he had attended, and when all had retired to their homes. Higgins, prowled the streets, where the better people lived. He came upon a ladder leaning against a house that allowed easy access to a bedroom window. Higgins climbed the ladder and peered through the curtain. He saw a young lady place her jewellery on the dressing table before retiring to bed, leaving a rush light burning. He returned to the house after the young lady was asleep and climbed through the window, took the jewellery from the table, unlocked the jewellery box and removed the contents and rifled some drawers, one of which creaked on opening.

'O Mary' said the young lady in her sleep, '*you know how tired I am; can't you put things straight in the morning?*' She was never to know how lucky she was. If she had opened her eyes he would have killed her on the spot. As it was, he held his breath, and when all became quiet again he made his escape with his ill-gotten gains. The following day, he joined in the hunt with his hounds, reading with the others the handbill account of the robbery and the substantial reward for the apprehension of the thief. With those around him he wondered how such a dastardly crime could have occurred while a young woman lay asleep. The reports of the time state that he was arrested and convicted, and at his trial he said, '*If that tired girl had risen up in bed and seen me, I should have murdered her on the spot*'. No record has been found as to the outcome of his trial.

On one dark rainy winter's night in 1764, he rode from Knutsford to Bristol and back in 48 hours, a distance of some 300 miles. To try to hide the noise of his horse from his neighbours on the brick path leading up to his stable he would cover the horse's feet with woollen stocks. This way his neighbours were not disturbed at his odd hours returning home. It was while in Bristol that he broke into Mrs Ruscombe's house and murdered her and her maidservant. At the time, suspicion fell on the baker and even on the local chimney sweep, but no one was ever charged. The crime remained unsolved until his confession on the gallows in 1767. Higgins had entered the house early in the morning and, being disturbed by the maid, he murdered her, and left her body on the stairs. No doubt the commotion disturbed Mrs Ruscombe and he murdered her in her bedroom.

Neighbours became suspicious when Mrs Ruscombe failed to appear in the morning and summoned the local constables. They broke into the house to discover the grizzly scene. At the time, Mrs Ruscombe had a considerable amount of money in the form of dollars in the house and this was missing. In 1810, some 43 years after the murder, neighbours at Knutsford recalled that at the time Higgins was spending a considerable amount of dollars. This was taken as confirmation that he was the murderer of Mrs Ruscombe and her maid, of College Green, Bristol in 1764.

Sometime after 1764, Higgins was in the Gloucester area and was once again under arrest by the constables of the area after breaking into a house. However, he escaped custody and with the constables in hot pursuit, he raced back north to Knutsford. This encounter forced him to move from the north of the country to the south. He now took up residence in an area described at the time as an expensive house in the French Hay (Frenchay) area of Bristol, safe with the knowledge that he had not been connected to the brutal murder of Mrs Ruscombe and her maid. By now his wife was fully aware of his profession, for it was she and her sister who forged the documents to try to obtain his release at Carmarthen in 1767.

Date of Execution Fixed

On 23rd October, the Sheriff received a warrant to execute Higgins and the date was set for 7th November. The sheriff read the order to Higgins. He received the information and his demeanour was described *'and it affected him greatly for a few minutes, but his spirits revived'.*

He said, *'I will get a reprieve before then'.*

A Bogus Respite

On the 23rd October Higgins wrote to his friends asking them to arrange for a reprieve. Accordingly, on 3rd November a respite duly arrived at the office of the Under Sheriff.

The document was a forgery; the document appeared to be in the handwriting of Lord Shelburne and initially it was accepted as being genuine. However, the Under Sheriff suspected that the respite was a sham when he discovered that the envelope used to deliver the letter carried a Brecon and a London postmark. He made enquiries only to find that the wife and sister of Higgins had dressed in white in order to disguise themselves and had delivered the respite to the Under Sheriff's office late in the evening. He made further enquiries, and is reported as saying *'for I do not want on my conscious the death of Higgins if the respite is genuine'.* Having been satisfied that the paperwork was a forgery, on the evening of 6th November he went to the gaol and told Higgins of his findings and that he should now prepare himself for the execution in the morning when he would be finally be sent into eternity.

The dawn approached and was bitterly cold as the crowds gathered outside the gaol and lined the route to the execution, which was to take place in public at Pensarn, a mile away from Carmarthen. A vast crowd greeted Higgins as he stepped out of the prison gate at 7 o'clock. Higgins walked so fast on his way to the gallows, via the old Roman Bridge, that the officials and spectators who were following had to run to keep up. As they walked and ran, they called the Under Sheriff a *'Scoundrel'*, shouting that the respite was real, and that he the Under Sheriff was taking away the life of a man with a reprieve in his pocket! The chanting continued for the whole journey to the public gallows at Babell Hill, Pensarn.

Higgins approached the gallows without a falter in his step and mounted the gallows. He had the appearance of a man without a care in the world, with a flower in his buttonhole, not at all like someone about to meet his maker. He looked about and settled his face upon the vast crowd assembled and proceeded to make a speech:

Gentlemen now is the time to do as you please. You have my reprieve in your custody.

Higgins prayed for 5 minutes and said to the waiting crowd:

I am ready.

He then handed a letter to the Under Sheriff. It not only contained his confession to the crime for which he was about to forfeit his life, but also several other crimes committed throughout the country. More startlingly, he confessed to the murder of Mrs Ruscombe, of College Green, Bristol, and that of her maidservant.

With that, the executioner kicked away the stool on which he was standing sending Higgins into eternity. However, that was not the end of his story. The crowds who had been calling the Under Sheriff *'a scoundrel'* were not to know that he had struck a deal with the local undertaker. The body was removed from the gallows almost immediately and not allowed to hang on the gallows for the customary hour in public. With the body removed to the undertaker's mortuary in Carmarthen and the apprentice set about to dissect the body. However, when they went to dissect the body Higgins was still alive and it was up to the apprentice to have the honour of giving him the *'coupe de grace'* and in so doing finishing the sentence of the law.

The undertaker made a cast of the body and had it on display in his private museum for many years. This anecdote finally put an end to the story the Notorious Lancashire Highwayman who passed through Carmarthen on his way to Laugharne and ended his life hung, dissected, and buried in the north side of St Peter's Church Carmarthen.

William Thomas   28th **March, 1770**

The execution of William Thomas at Pensarn is recorded in Spurrell's book. Spurrell does not give any details, either of the crime or the hanging and there are no newspaper accounts to tell the way William Thomas died, for the moment he remains a man of mystery.

Sioni'r Cornel   **1797**

Was a shoemaker he was hanged at Pensarn for the murder of his father. The execution is recorded in Williams Spurrell's account, but there are no further details

John Morris   **Saturday 21st April, 1804**

The Cambrian for 21st April, 1804 carried the report of the Carmarthen Session states that John Morris a 66-year-old grey-headed man had received the sentence of death for stealing a horse. The horse was the property of Evan Price. It also reported that in the same court an Ann Bramer had been sentenced to deportation for the theft of a pocket book containing five guineas, the property of Francis Francis, together with Martha Davies who was in court for the theft of three blankets the property of Benjamin Thomas. Both females were ordered to be transported for a period of seven years.

Between April and June John Morris received a respite in his sentence of death and numerous petitions were put before the court for the execution to be commuted to transportation or life in gaol but to no avail. On 19th May, the Cambrian reported that all attempts to save this man had failed and that he was to be executed in June.

It was on Saturday 23rd June, 1804 that The Cambrian carried the following article

Saturday last (16th June, 1804) John Morris was executed at Carmarthen for horse stealing. Great interest was made to save his life, but it proved unavailing. The unfortunate culprit has been accused of much levity of conduct while under sentence of death but we can state on good authority, that his behaviour since his trial, and at the place of execution, (Pensarn, Babell Hill) was such as became his unhappy situation.

'Let him that thinketh he standeth take heed lest he fall'

Rees Thomas Rees was brought up in the County of Carmarthen and executed for the murder of his sweetheart on Saturday 19th April, 1817. At the age of 26, he was described as an honest, honourable man, who occasionally preached for the Presbyterian chapel of the area of Llangadock. He stood charged with the murder of Elizabeth Jones, a 19-year-old from the same district.

Both came from respectable families and had been courting for some years. They had intended to marry but Elizabeth's parents had refused to give their consent. It was felt that she was too young, being only 19 and Rees 26. They had spoken of their intention to marry but with the consent not forthcoming, they had to delay the marriage. During this period of courtship, they had entered into a relationship and Elizabeth had become pregnant but with the continual refusal of consent by her parents, Elizabeth became very concerned about the social stigma associated with being pregnant, and being forced to raise a child out of wedlock.

Having heard that there was a medication that would help her to terminate the pregnancy, Elizabeth asked Rees to buy it for her. Rees agreed, and then travelled to Brecon to buy it. They then set about covering their shame by terminating the pregnancy and Rees administed the concoction to Elizabeth. Rees left the house at midnight and went straight home. Not long after, Elizabeth's sister, Gwenllian Jones was awoken by the groans coming from her sister. She described how she found her rolling about on the floor in agony. Her body had become swollen and blood was coming from her mouth. She helped to get her sister onto the bed and was able to question her as to the cause of her illness. Elizabeth was able to describe through her swollen lips how Rees had given her a grey medicine. She had immediately become ill and she had told Rees that he was killing her. With that she went on to tell her sister that he had just walked away. She was able to describe how the medication had burnt her throat like fire but Rees had forced her to swallow at least three amounts of the liquid. It was later found that the poison had been so strong that the throat had become ulcerated, her gums and cheeks had become so swollen that they had stuck to each other. Her teeth had become black and so loose that she was able to pull them out to show her mother. In this condition, she lasted a few hours before death was her salvation.

Rees had not gone home. He had started walking away from the area, intending to go to America to start a new life, but had decided to return to face the authorities in the hope that the outcome would be in his favour. He was arrested and brought before the court to answer the charge of murder. In his defence, he insisted that Elizabeth had swallowed numerous concoctions on the days before her death. He also stated that a number of Elizabeth's relatives had known about the pregnancy and that they had obtained various concoctions for her to take. Nevertheless, it was the evidence from Gwenllian that sealed his fate. Her evidence was considered that as being a dying declaration. Many witnesses came forward on behalf of Rees and all concurred that he had a previous excellent character. However, the Judge, Mr Justice Haywood, in his summing up directed the jury that their judgement must consider all the aspects of the case and urged them to fully consider all the circumstances.

The jury retired at eight in the evening to consider their verdict, and after two hours of deliberation, they returned to the silent courtroom and announced their verdict. Guilty!

Mr Justice Heywood, in what was described as a suitable admonitory address, pronounced the sentence as prescribed by law. Death by Execution. He stated that the execution was to take place on Saturday, 19th April, 1817 and that the body was then to be dissected. Rees returned to Carmarthen Gaol to await his fate.

It was reported that after Rees had been sentenced, he made a full and frank confession to Rev Mr Peter the Presbyterian chaplain and Rev Mr Cole of the Wesleyan Methodist Society. Rees admitted that he had given the medicine to Elizabeth. It had not been his intention to kill her. His only intention had been to prevent the pregnancy and in so doing save the shame that they would have to endure if the pregnancy had gone through.

The Day of Execution

On the morning of Saturday 19th April, 1817 Rees Thomas Rees was brought out of the gate of the gaol and placed in a chaise and carried through 10,000 spectators who had gathered to witness the execution, as Rees ascended the scaffold at Pensarn, the ministers started praying with the crowd joining in. Rees looked down on the crowd and joined in with the singing and rejoicing that was taking place. It lasted for an hour. Rees then addressed the crowd in a calm voice and recited a prayer:

O Lord, thou knowest that I am a great sinner.
But my heart is glad to think that thou hast mercy for the greatest sinner.

Thou gavest mercy to Messiah
Mary Magdalene was cleansed.
Thou didst save the thief on the cross.
Oh cleanse thou me! Cleanse me
Cleanse me from my sins.
I am found wanting in the balance in this world.
Oh for a sufficiency to stand in judgement!
Here the mercy of men faileth.
Here the help of all is ended.
Lord, Jesus receive my spirit.

When he had finished, the crowd was silent. Many of the women were crying. The handkerchief was placed over his eyes by the executioner. As he felt the steps on which he was standing start to move he cried out

Nawr ydw fi ar ochr tangnefedd pob hwyl yn crudo ar y yr arglwydd iesu I fyn ysbryd.

Now am I trembling on the borders of eternity – Farewell?

The body of Rees Thomas Rees was later dissected before burial as directed by the court.

In a story written into the account about Rees Thomas Rees the following teachings were made from the pulpit. The ministers of the day would stand in the pulpit, preach to the congregation, warning them to be on their guard to be sure that they or any relative would not follow Rees Thomas Rees. The following are verbatim accounts by preachers at the time:

1. That no one has anything to allege to his relatives. They had no hand in what he has done. None but foolish and inconsiderate persons will upbraid them that a relation of theirs has been executed. It would be good for all who are ready to bring up such accusations, to consider, that such a misfortune may befall some of their relations in like manner.

2. That it is a duty incumbent on all parents to pray that their children may be kept undefiled until death, as well as for grace to save them to everlasting life. Before Rees Thomas Rees had committed this melancholy deed, many were of opinion that he would have been a

renowned and useful man in his day. Together with teaching children to pray for 'deliverance from evil' it is necessary that parents should frequently pray to God for them and converse often with them about many ways that sin has to draw young people astray, how to escape the temptations, and the honour of ending their days without having their names polluted by crimes. There is reason to fear, that very few do conscientiously present their children to God's care. – Parents remember Rees Rees.

3. That one may be a member of a church, and be in a great esteem, and yet fall into shameful sins. What has happened to this young man calls loudly on those who stand to take heed lest they fall. Many will say, *'I will never go in the same path that he has gone.'* He had no intention of doing this, until he had been led astray by one thing and another. The fault was not on religion that he fell into this ditch. It is as unreasonable to say, owing to this man, Ah, such are all professors, as it would be to say, *All the mechanics of the kingdom are thieves,* because a mechanic has been executed for theft in such and such a place. And this melancholy circumstance will not be a scoff with any professors, but those who are glad to have every sect under dishonour, save their own sect. Every lover of religion would morn for this sad event. It would be good for encouraging us to pray to be undefiled until the end, – to remember Rees Rees.

4. That it is very dangerous to trifle with sin. Without a doubt this man's wicked heart, by tempting him to commit fornication, said unto him, *'Thou shalt marry, and then no one will ever come to know of this.'* And said also, after having failing to get married, *'thou hast no need to fear to give her what she wants to have, it will not endanger her life, it will certainly destroy her pregnancy, hundreds have given the same to their sweethearts, and no harm has happened'.* This narrative shews that one sin opens a door too many sins, and that small things become of great moment in the end. Let every one who may be tempted to commit this sin, --- remember Rees Rees.

5. That it is a very wicked habit for young men and women to be courting at untimely hours. In those places where this wicked custom prevails, fornication and uncleanness overspreads the country. It would be easy for heads of families, by practising their power, to put a stop to it. An hour or two, before bed time, would be sufficient for young men and women to converse with each other, and then let the

master of the house see that they separate, and that the door be locked. This sin will not be got the better of, until the churches see that this immodest mode of courtship is done away with among all those who profess the religion of Christ, – Head of families remember Rees Rees.

6. That it is when a young couple begin in their courtship, and not when they speak of marriage, parents should shew their dislike for such and such a one. If you are not willing that your son or daughter should be courting with a person you dislike, speak in proper time. Many, by preventing their children to get married when they wish, and in proper age, cause them to commit fornication. After they have fallen to this shameful sin, many parents say, *'They must be married now.'* Not now, but when they begged you permission, you ought to have been willing. It is not likely that this young man would have come to this untimely end if he should have had leave to marry the young woman when he solicited her parents' consent. – Parents remember Rees Rees.

William Baines   23rd **May, 1818**

It was in the year 1817 that the village of St Clears became the centre of attention for the whole principality. In the spring of 1817, a chaise stopped in the village outside the White Lion. From the chaise stepped a lady who was described as being 'of a superior appearance'. However, she was on crutches and accompanied by her son, William Baines two gentlemen and a young girl on horseback. The young girl it turned out was Jane Baines, the daughter and the two men were her nephews, Henry and Andrew Thomson.

They took up residence at the house known as White Cottage. Mrs Baines and her daughter become well known in the area, together with her nephews, who went by the name of Thomson. This was an alias. Their real names were Henry and Andrew Johnson. They displayed remarkable talents, elegance and a fascinating manner to such a degree that the daughter had everyone spell bound that encountered her. Miss Baines and the nephews entered into every part of society and frequented all the high society functions of the day.

However, Mrs Baines and her son remained at the house. This did not go unnoticed and the explanations were that the son was keen to perform chemical experiments, to which purpose a small-darkened room had been set aside. This room was close to the sitting room and Mrs Baines, it was said, was guarding this sanctuary. No one ever entered the room.

When he left the room it was always locked. William Baines never left the room and a walk at night was the only exercise that he appeared to take.

The large orders that they gave the local tradesmen become much sought after. However, the amount purchased was far in excess of the family needs and the local inhabitants were often given a saddle of mutton or a piece of beef or turkey in exchange for cash. Later it was found that they paid for the goods in forged bank notes and received real notes from their unsuspecting neighbours.

It was at this time that the bank in Carmarthen was finding that a large number of their bank notes were forged. The bank notes were described as being so well forged that the bank had great difficulty in detecting them. It was only with the discovery of two notes bearing the same number that the forgeries became known. At the same time, the Bank of England, in Carmarthen, was also suffering from fraud. A lawyer living in St Clears discovered who was making the forgeries. He reported to the Carmarthen bank that he had strong suspicion about a family in St Clears, who were classed as outsiders and whom all the resident's had become infatuated with. He was able to persuade one of the bank partners to spend a day with him at his sister's home, not far from the Baines's house. As they drove past the White Cottage Miss Baines and her cousin were out on the porch and as the carriage passed the lawyer and the bank partner thought that they saw alarm on the faces of the couple. After this, it would appear that the mysterious room within the house was now left open and a cleaner who entered the house reported that there was nothing in the room. Also, the family were reported as being busy at night in the garden. Mrs Baines covered up this change by saying that she had induced her son to give up his chemical pursuits as it was damaging his health, and that she was turning the room into a boudoir for her daughter. By this time, William Baines had already left the area and was living in Bath, seeking medical advice. The family now appeared to be packing and closing the house down and when asked by the neighbours, they were informed that they were going to join William in Bath.

It was in the November 1817, that they left St Clears to catch the mail stagecoach from Carmarthen to Bristol. It was at the Inn that one of those strange coincidences of life occurred and the result could not have been foreseen. One of the partners of the Carmarthen Bank, who had received a great number of the forged notes, was at the coach house waiting to catch the same stagecoach as Mrs Baines and her daughter. The partner was in the queue and as a £10 note was handed over as payment for the fare, he thought that he saw something strange in the note. Out of sight of the ladies he asked if he could examine it. He found that it was forgery and such a good forgery that if he had not been there it would have passed to the innkeeper as genuine.

The partner of the Bank of Carmarthen enquired about these two well dressed ladies and found that they had been spending a large amount of money in the local shops prior to leaving St Clears, always in bank notes. A warrant to arrest Mrs Baines and her daughter was obtained and they were found eating a hearty dinner, which had been paid for with forged Carmarthen Bank notes.

It was not until the 14th December that William Baines was arrested in Bristol. He had taken lodging at The Plume of Feathers, a public house in Bristol; in his possession was found a trunk and in the trunk was an engraved copper plate for a two pound note of the Governor and Company of the Bank of England, some unfinished notes and various tools used to counterfeit Bank of England notes. He was returned to Carmarthen to face trial on the Bristol to Milford Mail Stage Coach. By this time Andrew Johnson one of the cousins had also been arrested at Llandilo but it was not until Wednesday 1st April, 1818 that all four stood trial before Mr Justice Heywood.

The Trial
The four were charged with forging Bank of England bank notes. The evidence presented before the court was that constable Robert Harman arrested William Baines at the Plume of Feathers, a public house in Bristol, and found in the room bank notes and instruments for the use of counterfeiting Bank of England notes. William Baines had arrived at the Plume of Feathers and had requested a room of his own and the landlady in evidence stated that when he left the room he always locked it and took the key with him.

Thomas Thomas, a doctor in St Clears gave evidence that Andrew Johnson, alias Thompson, had requested that he explain in Welsh to William David, a carpenter in St Clears, the dimensions of a block roller and screw, which David was to make. William David identified his work to the court. Later William Davies, a carpenter in Carmarthen gave evidence that he had made a wooden box, which had later been joined to a piece of mahogany. This produced the watermark used in the Bank of England notes. Henry, Andrews's brother, was never brought to trial as no evidence could be found that he had passed forged notes.

Andrew Johnson, arrested at Llandovery, was found to be in possession of forged £2 notes and evidence was produced that he had been passing the forgeries in Llandilo on 9th December at the Bear Inn. He had presented the forgeries in the Ivy Bush at Carmarthen. When Joseph Henry Harper, an engraver at the bank examined the notes, he declared that they were the best that he had ever seen.

William Baines in his defence admitted to the forgeries saying that from an early age he had been interested in engraving and that the fabrication of the notes and subsequent use by his family was to hide an accident that he had had in his room at St Clears. He said that he had removed some £300 in notes from his mother bag to compare them to his own but had left a candle burning over them when he left the room for a short while. When he returned to the room, the candle had burnt the real notes and to hide his embarrassment he had substituted the real notes for the forgeries in the hope that his mother would not find out what had happened. Not long after he had left St Clears for Bristol and his mother, sister and cousin had used the forged notes unsuspectingly. Three witnesses giving evidence to the jury had stated that Johnson had an annual income of £400 following the death of his father in 1816 and that the family were well respected.

With this evidence, William Baines took the whole responsibility for the offence upon himself. He declared that his mother, sister and cousins knew nothing of his experiments in his private room and that he never discussed or disclosed any of his transactions to them. He stated that his real name was Kyle; he was the son of Elizabeth Baines by a former husband.

When the judge had finished summing up the evidence, the jury pronounced Baines guilty and Andrew Johnson not guilty. Mr Justice Haywood pronounced sentence of death on William Baines, giving him no hope of mercy, and imploring him to make the best use of the short time allotted to him on this side of the grave.

Elizabeth and Jane Baines pleaded guilty at the beginning of the trial on the understanding from the Bank that their sentence would be commuted to one of twelve-month imprisonment. Whilst in prison they were visited by friends who described them as having elegant manners. Jane Baines was seen as a classical beauty, with an interesting style of dress, which was a grey silk made in a Spanish fashion, a small velvet cap on one side of her head, a black lace veil falling over her figure. The gloom of the cell had been relieved by a landscape, drawn by Jane Baines on the cell wall with charcoal and a transparency to hide the cell bars. At the end of their sentence Mrs Baines walked unaided and without her crutches. No doubt this deception was no longer needed. Some years later Jane was seen in London at the Adelphi and it was later reported that she had gone to Switzerland as a governess, and later as a companion to the Countess of Florence. She later married a noble man and finally wore a coronet.

As for William Baines, he had to wait for his day of reckoning. The date was set as 23rd May, 1818, but even this was not without incident. On the eve of the execution, four prisoners attempted to escape. It was only with the vigilance of the keeper of the jail that the plot was discovered. He had received information of the escape attempt and that it was going to happen between midnight and one in the morning. He mustered assistance from the other warders and kept watch in a way that was described as being 'properly armed'. Four inmates had made a hole in the cell wall during the evening. This had taken them three hours to complete. The tools, a scissors a knife and rope, had been smuggled into the prison in a pitcher of broth that had been delivered during the day for one of the prisoners. They had intended to climb onto the roof of the hospital and, with the rope, climb over the wall of the jail and make good their escape. Of the four, three were awaiting transportation to the colonies for 14 years, one for stealing a cow and two for theft. The fourth was Baines, who was due for execution the following day. All four were apprehended in the grounds. The three were duly transported. As for Baines, the failure of the escape was put down to his abstracted habits preventing it success.

Described by the prison officials, as being in a world of his own he seemed to be suffering for the sake of his mother and sister. He elicited none of the interest and popularity they had acquired, whilst he displayed a nobler mind. They displayed selfishness, and want of affection and no common feelings even at his hour of execution.

Baines had offered the Bank of England a method by which forgery of their notes would have been impossible if they obtained for him a reprieve. His idea was that the operation of certain compounds, would assume a great variety of colour on the paper used for making bank notes – this would render forgery impossible. If reprieved he was prepared to continue to experiment to perfect his idea. The Bank of England declined his offer and on Saturday 23rd May, 1818, William Baines was executed. It was said at the time that he had died sorry for his sins and convulsed with horror at his dreadful situation. As he approach the scaffold he was asked if the forgery of local Carmarthen notes could be assigned to him? He replied:

Do not torment me with such a question; all other forgeries might as well be attributed to me.

With that, he was launched into eternity and was reported to be dead within four minutes.

David Evans   **Wednesday 16th September, 1829**

In the early 1800's murder was a crime that very few committed, for they knew the sentence of the court was, 'Death by Hanging'. Nevertheless, murder did occur and those who tried to hide from the law were brought to book, and despatched to meet their maker with haste. One such murder was that of Hannah Davies, described at the time as a crime so atrocious that the blood of the common man boiled at the very thought of the horrible deed that had been perpetrated in their midst. When the court doors were opened on that September morning to allow the public access for the trial, the public gallery was full to capacity within two minutes, with many more crowding the street outside.

The prisoner, David Evans stood in the dock charged with the murder of Hannah Davies. He presented an appearance of benevolence with what could only be described as a total disregard for the crime for which he was about to forfeit his life; he had offended the laws of the country and would have to pay the penalty. He stood in the dock showing no emotion and maintaining an air of complete indifference throughout the trial.

Hannah Davies was at the time of her death in the service of Mrs Ann Jones. On 13th June, 1829 Hannah had asked her employer for permission to visit her father who lived some 9 miles away. Hannah had been unwell during the past few weeks and felt that the change of air would do her good. After completing her daily tasks, she left the house sometime between eight and nine in the evening to walk over the mountain to her father's house.

Evans was a frequent visitor to the house and on one occasion during the time when Hannah was ill, he had stayed the night, even going on one occasion late at night to the doctor to get medicine. At the trial, Sarah Davies, Hannah's sister remembered that Evans was at the house during this time and Evans had shown a great concern about Hannah. Evans had even spoken to Sarah, a conversation that he later denied. It had been agreed that Hannah should go to her father's for the weekend and that he would meet her on the road and walk her over the mountain. During the past weeks, Evans had made his intentions known to Mrs Jones and Sarah about his feeling for Hannah and they were generally regarded as sweethearts, who in time would marry.

On that fateful Saturday evening, Hannah set out to walk over the mountain from Rhiwsaithbren to her father's home at Tanygar. At about 9 o'clock Mrs Maria Daniel, walking across a field called Cae Nelly'r Gweydd, a route well known by the locals, saw Hannah. The path ran through the field and came out on a footpath that led to Tirycwm. Mrs Daniel stated that she knew that Evans lived in Tirycwm and that Hannah would have to walk past the area. Some time later in the evening, Evans was later seen running in a field at Esgarfynwent. He appeared to be in an agitated state.

This was the last time that Hannah was seen alive. Her body was discovered on Sunday 14th June, 1829, in a stream on the Pencarreg Mountain at Cefnblaine between 11 and 12 o'clock by Mr Timothy Davies. He had come across the body lying in the brook and at first thought that she was sleeping and went to wake her. It was at this point that he discovered that she was not breathing and that there was blood in the water and on the bank leading to the stream. He described the scene and said that the body had been dragged to the stream from the road as he found blood on the road and in the grass leading to the stream. He ran for help to the local farm and returned to the scene with Eleanor Simon and a young lad called Evan Richards, a farm hand. It appeared that Hannah had met her fate on the road as the marks on her body showed that she had fallen there having been struck about the head several times and her body dragged to the stream in an attempt to conceal it.

At the coroner's inquest, it was stated that Hannah was two to three months pregnant, and that she had died from several wounds. The coroner observed that two wounds in the neck had completely cut the neck to a depth of 3½ inches and that the spinal cord had been severed. Either of these wounds would produce instant death. From the extent of the wounds it appeared that, an axe or meat cleaver would have been the murder weapon. The axe or cleaver were quite common tools and could be found in any peasant's cottage at the time. The weather conditions on Sunday 14th June were described as being quite warm and dry. The coroner was able to therefore estimate the time of death to be about 11 o'clock the previous evening. This was about the time that Mrs Daniel saw Evans running.

Evans was questioned at his home on the day of the murder. He stated that he had not seen the girl for several weeks. This was a clear lie. He had been seen in her company on the day before the murder and had agreed to meet and walk Hannah over the mountain on the Saturday. In addition, footprints at the scene of the murder were the same as shoes found at Evans's house. His sister was in the house when the police arrived and was heard to say '*O David see where thou wast last night I hope thou art free from her'.* This was said before any mention of the murder was made. Evans said to his sister, *'I am, I know nothing about her, if I had to answer to God in judgement this moment.'*

At the trial Evans was asked how he earned his bread. He replied that he worked in the woods and that he had left his work on the Saturday evening about eight in the evening and that he had gone straight home. Asked about when he had last seen Hannah, Evans said that it was last Thursday. He said that he had no knowledge of her going to her fathers on the Saturday evening and she had not told him that she was pregnant. With that Sarah; Hannah's sister jumped to her feet and shouted *'You villain! How can you say she did not tell you so, – she did tell you so; and you asked her to wait a month longer to know if she was really pregnant:'* Evans then said to the court, *'Perhaps she did tell me once.'*

Throughout the trial, Evans maintained his innocence, even when addressed by the Judge; – *'David Evans the case against you is now closed, and this is the time for you to make your defence to the jury'.* Evans replied, *'All I have to say is that I am not guilty'.*

At the end of the trial the Judge, in an impartial manner, summed up the evidence and the jury retired for an hour and returned a verdict of 'Guilty'. The Judge donned the black cap and passed sentence. The whole court, as well as the Judge, were clearly affected by the proceedings. Evans was the only one who seemed to have little regard to the proceedings and appeared quite unmoved. Evans was convicted at the Carmarthen Great Sessions on 16th September, 1829 and sentenced to a public execution.

The Confession

'This is the confession of me, David Evans, who am justly condemned to suffer, for committing a great offence against the laws of God and man. I die in charity with all men; I forgive all who may have offended or injured me, and I hope that all whom I might have injured in word or deed will forgive me also. I was received by Hannah Davies as her lover, and was much attached to her; I visited her on Thursday, the 11th June last, and remained in her company on that occasion about two hours, and before we parted she asked me, if she were to go to her father's house the following Saturday, would I accompany her on the road near Esgar Fynwent. I left home between nine and ten o'clock and took a billhook with me and told my sister that I was going to mend some gaps in the hedge; I began my work, but before I finished closing the gap, Hannah Davies came and called me, and asked if I was coming; my answer was that I would rather not

61

that night, and gave as an excuse that my sister was washing my stockings. She said, 'come this night, or I will never forgive you.' On this I went and proceeded along the road to Cwmsifigw, in the parish of Llanybyther. We then went over the mountain, and proceeded along in a friendly manner until we reached the spot where the murder was perpetrated. As we were passing the small hollow where the body was found, I struck her with the billhook, which was concealed under my coat, across her neck. She did not fall to the ground on the first blow; a second which I immediately dealt, brought her to the ground, but on what part of the body it fell, I cannot exactly say, nor how many more blows I gave, for I was bewildered, and almost frantic, and scarcely knew what I was doing. I was instantly smitten by my conscience after striking the first blow, and was sorry for the act; but I was urged to finish the deed for fear she would recover, and that the attempt would be discovered, and I suffer for it. I did not drag her from the road to the ravine, but she fell, I should think in that direction from the force of the blows. I then ran homewards as fast as I could, and on the way dipped the billhook in a pool of water, to wash away the blood. I reached home about one or two o'clock on the Sunday morning, and got to bed very silently, where I lay about an hour; I then got up, wiped my shoes, and put grease on them. These were the shoes produced at the trial. Upon leaving the house on Saturday I told my sister, to prevent her coming out of the house, that she not see me going with Hannah Davies, that I would drive the cattle into the night field; and in order to deceive her further, I finished mending the gaps in the hedges, after I got up on the Sunday morning. I do not think my sister heard me coming into the house, for I came in as silently as I could, and she was in bed. There was no blood on my cloths, and I had no accomplice whatever in committing the murder. I was instigated to this dreadful act by a feeling of jealously, and I earnestly implore all young men to take warning by my melancholy, and not give way to unruly passions, I return my most sincere thanks to those, in whose charge I have been ever since the awful and just sentence of the law was imposed against me, for the very humane and tender kindness and attention, spiritual and temporal, which I received from them.'

'DAVID EVANS'

This confession was delivered voluntarily by the prisoner in Welsh and translated by

Thomas Jones, Chaplain of Carmarthen Gaol. 1829

The Execution

On Monday 21st September, 1829, 10,000 spectators assembled outside the gaol for the public execution of David Evans. The scaffold had been erected on a platform raised inside and above the front wall of the Gaol facing Spilman Street. As the day approached, the murderer turned to the church for redemption. His victim had walked unsuspecting to her death. First he had seduced her and then hurried her 'with all her imperfections on her head,' into the hands of her creator. So swift was death, that she was unable to utter a cry for help. His death was not to be so swift. He had time to dwell on the circumstances of his crime and in so doing, he made a full and frank confession to the Rev Jones, Chaplain of the County Gaol.

At 9 o'clock, the High Sheriff arrived at the gaol and the procession was lined and preceded to walk to the scaffold. EVANS ascended the steps with a firm walk and positioned on a mark over the drop. The agreed signal was a dropping of a handkerchief. However, when the handkerchief fell the trapdoor opened, the beam holding Evans collapsed, and the crowd uttered a loud groan. Evans fell to the ground in a heap and appeared to be unhurt. Evans now was expecting his life to be spared, for he believed that as the first attempt to hang him had failed, then he could not be re-hung. He shouted in broken English

No hang again, No! No! No! Gentleman was hung twice for the same thing.

He then continued to shout in Welsh about undergoing a second punishment for the same offence. He begged all about to help him. He claimed that he had escaped the first death. He continued to shout and struggle while the Governor explained that the sentence of death had to be carried out. The beam was quickly replaced, and the process continued. Evans accepted his fate and ascended the scaffold for the second time. The noose was placed about his head and he was sent into eternity. He was left suspended for one hour and when the body was removed it was dissected and placed in an open coffin for the public to inspect. They came in their thousands to see the fate of the murderer of Hannah Davies and the dissected remains of her lover, David Evans.

William Spurrell records the executioner as being a pensioner from Worcester. David Evans was the last man to suffer the fate of dissection in Carmarthen.

It was around 10.30 on 12th November, 1887, a cold winters morning, that Thomas Davies, a messenger at the Dafen Tinworks in Llanelli was found dying, in a field he had been brutally battered about the head on Bryngwyn Hill. Near to the scene, covered in blood, police found a hanger, a tool used in the local tinworks. Thomas Davies had been carrying a bag containing the wages for the tinworks, £590 in gold and silver, of which £300 was missing.

It was in the evening of the same day that the police went to question Rees at his home and, as a result, David Rees was arrested on suspicion of having committed the murder. It was widely believed at the time that there was another man involved in the crime. Witnesses had reported seeing another man in the area but despite extensive police enquiries only Rees stood in the dock.

The evidence against Rees was very comprehensive. A young boy by the name of W.J. Lewis came forward and told the police that he had been hiding in the hedge overlooking the murder scene. He was later able to identify Rees to the police. It was this boy who first spoke of the second man. If there was another person involved, Rees was to take his identity to the grave.

As to the motive for the crime, it was one of robbery. It was well known that Thomas Davies carried large amounts of money from Llanelli to Dafen. Rees was also well known in the area and for some days before the murder, he had been asking various people for a loan. On 2nd November, he had asked the Rev Phillips for £20. On 6th November, he had asked David Thomas for £5 and on another occasion 50 shillings from David Samuel. All had refused to lend any money.

What was considered at the time to be the most damming piece of evidence came from a Mrs Hughes of the Tremelyn Inn, Llanelli. She stated that on 31st October, she had had a long conversation with Rees, and it was during this conversation that he threatened to kill her because she had refused to lend him money. The defence tried to say that this was a joke and that Rees had no intention of carrying out the act. Nevertheless, 12 days later 'Tom Bach' was beaten about the head and left to die in a field. No doubt the thought of 'Tom Bach' walking on this lonely path with such a large amount of money and not giving it up without a fight must have occurred to Rees, as in his hand he had gone prepared to use force, carrying the hanger.

Frederick Hopkins lived in the same road as Rees and gave evidence that he had met Rees on the road to Dafen at about 10.00 a.m. in the morning. Rees had gone through the fields to Box Cemetery. This Rees

Male warder, 1900's

Prisoner being photographed unwillingly

The screw

Record Book, 1931

Photo's from Felons Register
(Courtesy of Carmarthen County Archives)

Straight jacket

Stocks

Box stocks

Strait jackets

Female Warder, circa 1900

Record Book, 1898

Governor's Bible

Shackles dated 1935 – used to shackle females

Body belt

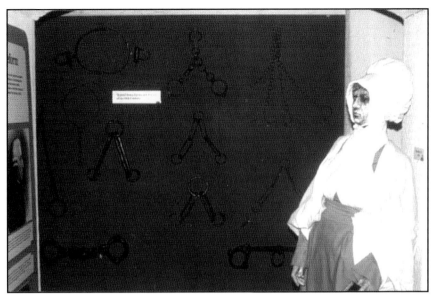

Various irons

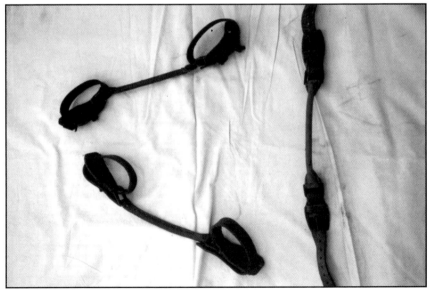

Female hand cuffs

70

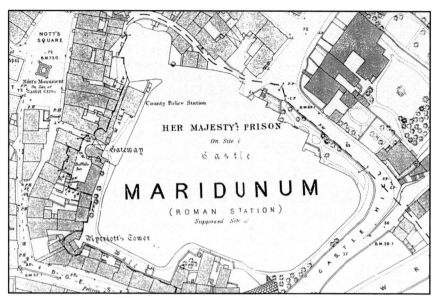

(Courtesy of Carmarthen County Archives)

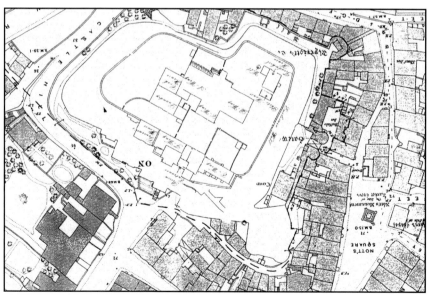

Block plan of 1898 superimposed on Castle site

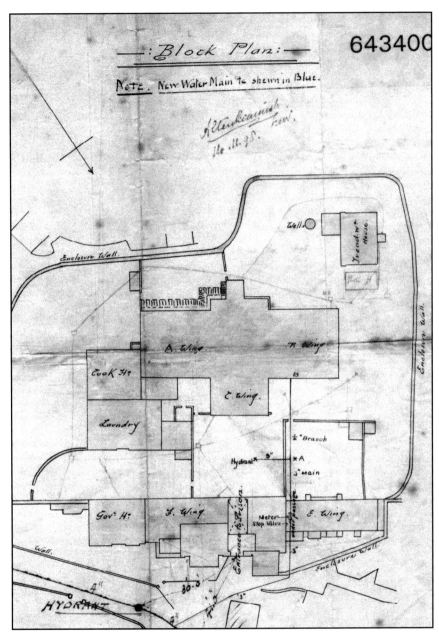

Carmarthen Prison – Block Plan

(Courtesy of Carmarthen County Archives)

Treadwheel
(Courtesy of Senior Officer Brian White, retired HMP Gloucester)

HMP Carmarthen – Mary Jane Hughes at Gate, circa 1922
(Courtesy of Mr Glyn Lewis, retired officer HMP Swansea)

Warder James Hughes, circa 1922
(Courtesy of Mr Glyn Lewis,
retired officer HMP Swansea)

Bridge Street and Carmarthen Gaol from
the air, c. 1930. The castle keep, gatehouse
and parts of the wall and the south-west
corner tower show quite clearly. Coracle
Way now cuts through the houses and
streets at the bottom of the photograph
(Courtesy of Carmarthen County Archives)

Warders at Carmarthen prior to closure
(Courtesy of Mr Glyn Lewis, retired officer HMP Swansea)

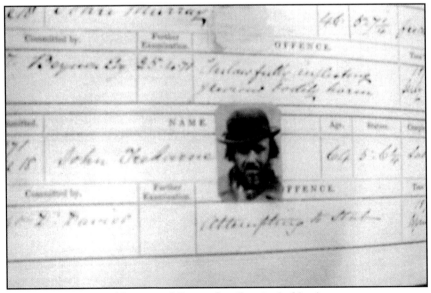

(Courtesy of Carmarthen County Archives)

Old prison wall adjoining County Hall

Inkpots, quill, ivory letter opener. Property of Mr Glyn Lewis,
retired officer HMP Swansea

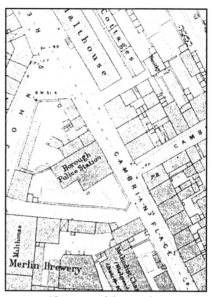

John Nash (source unknown)

(Courtesy of Carmarthen County Archives)

The Castle

Hanes Llofruddiaeth Druenus

HANNAH ·· DAVIES,

Ar Fynydd Pencareg, yn swydd Gaerfyrddin.

Cafodd Dafydd Evans ei grogi yn Ngharchar Caer-
fyrddin Medi 21ain, 1829, am lofruddio ei gariad-ferch,
Hannah Davies. Cyflawawyd y weithred anfad ar nos
Sadwrn, Mehefin 13eg, yn yr un flwyddyn, a deuwyd o hyd
i gorff briwedig y ferch anffodus ar Fynydd Pencareg gan
rai pobl ar eu ffordd i le o addoliad y boreu canlynol,
mewn afonig fechan, dyfroedd yr hon oeddynt wedi eu
lliwio gan ei gwaed am tua dwy filldir. Cafodd y carcharor
ei brofi o flaen yr Ynad Goulbourn, ar y 15fed o Fedi;
dedfrydwyd ef am tua 11 o'r gloch y nos, a chyn y wawr
darfu iddo gyfaddef ei euogrwydd wrth ddau gwnstabl
oeddynt yn gofalu am dano.

---

1 RIGOLION Sir Gaerfyrddin, .
    Ac Aberteifi wiw,   .
A phawb o'r Cymry mwynion
   Sy'n rhodio ar dir y byw,
Gwrandewch ar byn o hanes
   Truanus i'w goffhau,
Sy'n rhybudd mawr i'r ie'nctyd,
   Ac hefyd i bob rhai.

'Nol magu plant yn anwyl,
   A'u meithrin fore a hwyr,
Pa beth ddaw i'w cyfarfod,
   'Does neb ond Duw a wyr,
Ond gweddïwn ar yr Arglwydd,
   I'w cadw rhag y Fall,
Nis gwyddom beth ddaw iddynt,
   O lore hyd y llall.

'R oedd merch yn mhlwyf Pencareg,
   Yn swydd Gaerfyrddin fawr,
A i henw Hannah Davies,
   Boed byshys i chwi 'nawr ;   .

A hono mewn gwasanaeth
   Yn barchus iawn yn bod,
Yn caru â mab ieuanc
   O gwmpas ugain oed.

Ond pryfio wnaeth yn faichiog,
   Fel llawer gyda hi,
A thraethu wnaeth i'w chariad,
   " Yn faichiog yr wyf fi ; "
A gofyn wnaeth i'w meistres,
   A gni hi ganiatad
'Fynd adref ar nos Sadwrn,
   I wel'd ei mam a'i thad.

A'i meistres a ddywedai,
   " O brysia, gwna dy waith,
Cai fyn'd brvdnawn yn gynar,
   Wyth milltir sydd yn faith : "
Atebai Hannah'n dirion
   A mwynaidd iddi hi,
" Nid af fi ddim mor gynar,
   Mae cwm'ni gydaf fi."

Ond yn yr hwyr cychwynodd,
   I fyn'd tua thy ei thad,
Heb feddwl fod ei chwmp'ni
   O fwriad gwnaeyd ei brad ?
Ac yna boreu dranoeth,
   Rhyw ffermwr ddaeth yn fwyn
I edrych am ei ddiloedd,
   Ei ddefaid oll a'i ŵyn.

1829 (source unknown)

78

The Western Mail, circa 1920

The Western Mail, circa 1920

Sir Eric Geddes, Chairman of the Economy Committee, will not speak on the report in Parliament, for he has completed plans to go to the Pyrenees.

The Western Mail, circa 1920

SOMEBODY PLEASED.

BILL SIKES: It strikes me, Bill, that this 'ere Geddes is a bloke as ought to be encouraged.

The Western Mail, circa 1920

80

denied to the police. Rees had told Hopkins that he wanted to meet the post boy, as he wanted to collect a letter from him. Later it was established that he did indeed meet the post boy, Charles William Jones, on the old road to the cemetery. Rees and Hopkins went as far as Cae Cotton, where the road forked, Rees saying that he wanted to get a shave and have his shoes nailed. This was about a quarter past ten. Police constable, Daniel and Mrs Anne Williams next saw Rees at the old slaughterhouse at about twenty past ten. They gave evidence that they saw him crossing the road at the Box tramway.

Tom 'Bach' Davies arrived at the bank to cash the cheque in exchange for the wages for the workers. PC McCoy later reported seeing Tom Davies walking towards the Dafen Tinworks shortly before eleven. Then Elizabeth Simpson met both Rees and Davies going towards Dafen sometime between half past ten and eleven. First, she saw Rees by the milestone near Fulford's garden and then Davies by the Boar's Head. The Master of the Workhouse also saw the two men at 10.47 and 10.58 respectively.

Another vital piece of evidence came from other boys playing in the field. The first was a boy called Rosser; who was on his way to the workhouse when he met Samuel Thomas and David Samuel John. They were swinging on the gate. As Rosser walked into the field, he met Rees walking coming towards him. Rees asked him who the boys were on the gate and Rosser replied 'Thomas and John'. John later recalled seeing Rees and Rosser talking in the field. Rees approached the boys on the gate, asked about the post boy, and told the boys to go home. One other boy, W.J. Lewis said he was in an adjoining field collecting dandelions for his rabbit. The times that he gave were unreliable. He did not have a watch and could only guess at the time of day. All that is known is that he returned to his grandmother's house sometime between twelve and one.

Young Lewis was unable to give an accurate time when he was in the field, but his account and later identification of the murderer was enough. A more accurate witness concerning the time was the relief officer of the tinworks; Mr David Jones. It was Dai Jones who described the second man in the area between 11.20 and 11.30. He described this man as being short and dark, and he seemed to be in a hurry between Capel Road and Coed Cae. With the three independent witnesses and the boy Lewis, who witnessed the murder, the police interviewed Rees at his home. At first, he denied using the Cemetery Road and even went on to say that he had not been to the Dafen Tinworks for five weeks. As a result, of the police questioning, Rees was arrested and charged with the murder of Thomas Davies. In answer to his denial of being in the area and going to the works, the prosecution at his trial was able to produce several witnesses to the fact that Rees was seen at the works on the night before the murder and he was seen in the room where the hanger was kept.

Having heard the evidence the jury retired and returned a verdict after 32 minutes – *'Guilty'*. Rees made no reply when asked if he had anything to say before being sentenced. With great solemnity the judge placed the black cap upon his head and passed the sentence of death.

The prisoner was then removed from the dock and taken to the cells below. Then something unprecedented in the annals of court proceedings occurred. Rees started to shout and complain that he had not understood the sentence or even the fact that he had been condemned to die. On hearing this, the Governor of the gaol Mr O. Thomas, who was present in the court, went to speak to the Judge. The Judge returned to the Bench and without donning the black cap ordered that the prisoner be brought back into court. He repeated the sentence of the court and requested that the interpreter, Mr Long Price, translate the sentence into Welsh. As the prisoner was led away for the second time Mr Price broke down crying as did many other at the repetition of the solemn scene. This closed what was at the time described as a most remarkable trial. It had lasted 2½ days, a total of 23 hours sitting time.

Members of the church visited Rees at Carmarthen Prison and described him as having lost his old sparkle. When they asked him how he was, he replied in Welsh – *'Picwl trist'* [sad pickle]. In further conversation, Rees went on to say, *'I am innocent, and have been wrongly convicted,'* but that he would rather be there in those circumstances than have that crime on his conscience. His words were; *'Ond mae'n well gen i fod yma ar gam na bod yma yn euog.'* Reminded of the confession that he had already made, he replied emphatically that he was not guilty of the murder, and had nothing further to say about it. He had said all he had to say on the matter, and added he was glad he did not kill Davies, laying great emphasize on the word 'Kill'. Being asked who did kill 'Tom Bach', Rees replied, *'Dyna beth sy yn dywyll i fi, syr.'* [That is the dark side of me, sir.] The members of the church pressed for him to reveal his accomplice but his only reply was *'Hum'*. This was the only indication by Rees that he was shielding another and that he was prepared to go to the gallows with that knowledge. As they left the cell for the final time his parting words were, *'They all know me in Llanelli. Remember me to them'*.

The Confession

I, David Rees, confess with much grief and sorrow that on the 12th day of November, 1887, I myself, single-handed, and unaided by any other person, did wilfully kill Thomas Davies, of Felinfeol, Llanelli. The money which I took away from the possession of the said Thomas Davies I afterwards hid somewhere in some hedge of the field next adjoining the Box Cemetery, but I cannot at present remember the exact spot. I wish to state that drink was the cause of all this. I was drunk at the time I committed the crime, but I felt muddled in consequence of my having been drinking heavily during the previous day and night. I am truly sorry for what I have done and I humbly entreat the forgiveness of the deceased relatives for the misery and grief I have caused them. What I have stated above is a true confession, and I have made this confession as being the only reparation and satisfaction I can offer to those I have so grievously wronged, and may the Lord have mercy on my soul.

(Signed): David Rees, Dafen.
Witnessed O. Thomas, Governor.
T.R. Walters, Chaplain.

The Execution

Tuesday 13th March, 1888, was the day fixed for the execution of David Rees. Rees appeared to sleep well during the night and awoke at about 5.45 a.m. He got up and dressed without prompting. At 6.30 a.m., a breakfast was delivered to the condemned cell. It consisted of bread, milk and butter. He refused tea. At 7.00 a.m., the prison Chaplain, Rev T.R. Walters entered the cell and offered spiritual comfort. All was quiet in the gaol until 7.45 a.m. It was at this time that the prison bell started to toll, announcing to all within and without, that the execution was about to take place. Berry the executioner entered the cell 7.57 a.m. carrying the pinioning straps.

With a weight of 11 stone, a drop of 6 feet was allowed. It was explained to the reporters present that the executioner had calculated the drop to allow the rope to exercise a strain of 27 cwt. This it was explained as being the same calculations used to execute Nash, the Swansea Murderer [11th December, 1886].

Timing was important and at 7.57 a.m., Berry pinioned the prisoner. By this time, Rees was crying bitterly. At one minute to eight, the procession started from the condemned cell to the scaffold. First came the Chief Warder and Warder Jones; then the Chaplain reading the Burial Service; the condemned man had to be supported by Warders Howells and Thomas; followed by the executioner; The Under-Sheriff Mr D. Long Price; the prison Surgeon Mr James Rowland and the Governor Mr O.

Thomas. The reporters closely followed the procession, they representing the many newspapers of South, West and Mid. Wales.

Rees was in such a state that he had to be supported as he walked by the warders at his side. He was sobbing bitterly as the procession made its way across the yard to the execution shed. During his time in prison Rees had put on weight. This was a common occurrence in prisoners awaiting execution and became known as *'Grief Fat'*. The extra weight did not go unnoticed by the assembled reporters.

The procession reached the shed in which the scaffold had been erected. Rees and the warders supporting him entered the shed followed by the Executioner. Rees was then positioned by Berry on the trap, the white cap placed over his head, and the rope adjusted around his neck. Finally, by placing the brass-locking ring under the left ear, the noose was in position. During all this time, the chaplain had continued to read the Burial service in Welsh with Rees repeating verses and shaking his head as if bewailing his terrible fate. At exactly one minute past eight as the chaplain read *'Arglwydd, bydd drugarog wrthym ni'*, the lever was pulled. The drop fell and Rees was launched into eternity. The process had taken half a minute from the time he had stood on the trap. As the drop fell open, the black flag was hoisted on the prison flagstaff above the female wards facing Spilman Street.

The scaffold was not new; it was reported at the time as being previously been used in Dolgelly at the execution of Cadwalladr Jones, executed for the murder of a woman in 1877. The depth of the pit was recorded as being ten foot with a clearance of seven foot to the crossbeam. Berry commented, *'It is the best I had ever seen'*. The rope used by Berry was Italian silk hemp; it had been used on four previous occasions by Berry, the last being Dr Cross at Cork on 10th January, 1888.

As for the crowd outside, they waited in silence for the black flag to be hoisted and the customary notice of execution to be posted on the gate. In the silence of the gaol the Chaplains voice could be heard in the prison yard, reading the service. The burial took place in the prison grounds in a grave dug in the prison garden on the northwest side of the prison.

As for the executioner, at 9.00 a.m., after he had removed the body from the scaffold, he went into the town and walked about unmolested. Curious young men followed him around town. On his return to the gaol at 9.45 a.m., he collected his bag and walked to the Carmarthen, London and North Western train station, where he boarded the 10.25 a.m., to Manchester. As the train moved of a cheer went up and Berry leaning out of the carriage window raised his hat and waved to the crowd. So, ended the final day of David Rees, the murderer who with an unknown accomplice murdered 'Tom Bach' of Dafen.

George Thomas   13th February, 1894

It was at 9.45 p.m. 19th November, 1893, that George Thomas approached Police Sergeant James Jones who was patrolling King Street Carmarthen, with news that was to shock the whole community.

Little did Sergeant Jones know that when he took Thomas to one side that the statement was to prove so terrible. Thomas immediately confessed to killing a young girl and that he had left the body near the 'Joint Counties Lunatic Asylum'. At first, the sergeant could not believe what he was hearing and continued to question the unhappy man. Thomas insisted that what he had said was the truth, and was taken to the police station. It was then, in the lights of the station, that blood stains could be seen on Thomas's hands and cloths.

The police immediately went to the area indicated by Thomas and about a quarter of a mile away from the asylum, midway between Pentremaurig Farm and the small cottage Dawelan, the searchers came across the body of a young girl lying in a pool of blood. She had two gaping gashes in the throat, and her head had almost been severed from her body. One of the wounds had started from the ear and crossed the jawbone to the cheek, whilst the other, described as a clean cut across the throat, severed the windpipe. The murder weapon, found nearby, was described as being a long black handled razor. The authorities decided to quickly remove the body to the mortuary before the town folk awoke in the morning.

At the time, no motive could be found for the murder. Thomas was a 25-year-old who had just left the army. The murdered girl, identified as being that of Mary Jane Jones, aged 15½, was described as being an exceptionally pretty young woman, who lived with her aunt, Mrs Rosie Dyer at the cottage Dawelan, near to where the body was found. Later as the evidence began to unfold it would appear that the girl had been seen in the company of Thomas on many occasions and had grown tired of him and was now avoiding him. In a fit of rage he had followed and killed her.

George Thomas became known as 'the self condemned man'. He was described as muscular, with light complexion. A native of Johnstown he came from a very respectable family and had many relatives living in the neighbourhood. His father John Thomas was a pattern maker at the Old Foundry in Carmarthen.

On the night of the murder Thomas was seen running at twenty minutes to ten near the Fusiliers Monument, in Lammas Street. Thomas approached PC T. Jones and just stood looking at the constable before running away. Next, he was seen running hastily through Guildhall Square and Nott Square and it was here, at a quarter to ten that he approached Sergeant Jones and made his confession. The newspaper report at the time printed the words:

'Confession is good for the soul'

During the night, the police called at the home of Mrs Dyer but decided, when they saw how feeble she was, to tell her that her niece had broken her leg and that she had been taken to the infirmary. Alas, what a different tale she was to hear in the morning.

Johnstown, was a suburb of Carmarthen, about a quarter of a mile on the main road from the Obelisk set up to the memory of General Picton. About the same distance from Johnstown on the rising ground to the north, the Joint Counties Asylum stood in its own enclosed grounds, with a country road skirting the boundary. Following this road from the Asylum Lodge gate a lane turned to the left and crossing a small bridge is the cottage of Mrs Dyer, described as a pretty homestead embossed in trees and shrubbery. The farmhouse of Pentremeurig was between the cottage and the asylum. With the close proximity of the Asylum, the area described as being lonely and fearsome at night. At 9.00 o'clock on the 19th November, in the rain sodden lane, and with the shadows of the hedge deepening the gloom, Thomas could work his will at leisure. Sunday was a good night to carry out the cowardly deed. A hurricane had been sweeping the country, and with the hundreds of poor demented creatures locked up in the asylum, a shriek of agony would have gone unnoticed. Even if it had been heard, strange cries were a common thing in the area of the lunatic asylum.

The Doctors report
In describing the young girl's condition, Dr Thomas's words, are worth recording:

'It was a fearful sight, I examined her and found a tremendous gash extending from the angle of the jaw towards the symphysis of the jaw three inches long and reaching the bone. In my opinion, this was the first wound inflicted. On further examination, I found another wound four inches and a quarter long, and extending from the left of the middle line of the front of the neck across the trachea. All the blood vessels were severed. In fact, the neck

was cut down to the vertebral column. Death must have resulted almost immediately after the infliction of the wound.'

'There must have been a terrible struggle, for the tips of the fingers were cut all to pieces by her attempting to clutch the razor with which the crime was committed and her right thumb was almost severed. It was the most awful sight I have ever seen.'

When asked for an opinion as to how the murderer hacked the victim to death the doctor replied.

'It has been told to me that he has admitted that after the first stroke he knelt on her and inflicted the second gash, but you must understand that this is only what I have heard. I have no positive evidence of it. I think, however, that he must have stood behind her and held her head with his left arm and inflicted the wounds with the right. He may have butchered her afterwards. I believe that he did.'

Thomas's Movements

On the fateful Sunday evening, Thomas was in the Lammas Street Chapel. He appeared uneasy throughout the service. No doubt, the razor was in his pocket and he was already planning the evil deed. A young servant girl was sitting next to him during the service and Thomas continually asked the girl the time, leaving the building before the end of the service.

On Sunday afternoon, Mary Jane was going to meet her friend Mary Morris at the Cooper's Arms, to have tea with her. She told her friend that she had seen Thomas near to the asylum on her way to Carmarthen and he had grabbed her saying, *'Give me a sweet kiss'*. He then caught hold of her and kissed her. Thomas was very much besotted with Mary Jane and had made his feelings known on many occasions. She, in return reciprocated none of that love, but openly discouraged it. In fact, she was very afraid of Thomas and her great aunt had noticed this.

The two friends spent the afternoon and evening together. Mary Morris last saw Mary Jane alive at about twenty minutes to eight. Mary Jane left to meet her brother David, a lad of 13 years of age, who was waiting for her at her other aunt's house, a Mrs Ann Phillips who lived next door to the Royal Oak Inn. Mary Jane had supper with her aunt and about eight thirty set off home with David. They walked up the lane leading to the asylum, and, after going, some distance her brother walked on to the house. Mary Jane for some unknown reason walked on and past

Pentremaurig Farm. Mrs Scurlock was standing in the door way and Mary Jane Jones called cheerfully *'Good night Rachel.'* These were the last word she was to say; a few moments later she was accosted by Thomas and met her doom.

Mary Jane was a good-looking, dark complexioned, intelligent young girl popular with her neighbours and friends. She had come to live in Carmarthen when her great aunt's husband had died. Her parents lived near the Joiners Arms, Fforestfach, Swansea; and her father was a weaver. Coming from a family of nine her aunt had offered to help the family by taking Mary Jane. She had proved a great help to her elderly aunt by collecting the rents to the numerous properties that she had in the town.

The police told Mrs Dyer of the murder the following morning and the first words she said were:

'O fy ngeneth fach? Beth wna i? Fyddai'n chwech deg saith os byddai fyw i weled yfory. Ond beth yw pwrpas byw.' 'Oh, my poor girl! What shall I do? I shall be 67 if I live to see tomorrow. But what is the use of living.'

'Pam na sbarith ei bywyd hi? Y ferch druan', 'Why did he not spare her life? My poor girl.'

Mrs Dyer stated that she knew George Thomas was saying in the town and that he believed he was courting Mary Jane. Mrs Dyer knew from her niece that this was not the case and that she spurned his affections. However, at the time she was not seeing any other boys.

Mrs Dyer was a widow Mary Jane had lived with her for just over a year. Thomas had begun coming to the house for about a fortnight before the murder. On one visit Mrs Dyer was able to describe how Thomas had tried to walk into the house to fetch water. As he approached the door he said to Mrs Dyer *'I am going to fetch water'*, but Mrs Dyer was not taken in with his boldness. She told him *'Stand where you are; don't come any further'*. Mary Jane, who was in the house at the time, handed Mrs Dyer the glass of water, and Mrs Dyer could see that Mary Jane was trembling at the thought of this man at the door. Mrs Dyer had known the Thomas family for over twenty years.

George Thomas

George Thomas, a 25-year-old army reservist, had served seven years in the Royal Artillery. Having been discharged from Fort Efford, Plymouth in August he had been unemployed and had not looked for any work. Before enlisting in the army, he had gone to the Model School and was described as a bright boy. After school he had worked as a messenger at Mr W.R. Edwards Emporium. His father, John Thomas, worked as a pattern maker at the Old Foundry in Blue Street for 40 years and was well respected in the community. George Thomas was one of ten children five girls and five boys. He was due to finish as a reservist on 22nd September, 1898. Upon leaving the army, he had started to drink heavily. His father stated that on leaving the Army Thomas had received a payment of £20 and that he had squandered the money without giving a single penny to his parents. In a statement, his father said; -

'He must have been mad when he did it, there is no insanity in my family. They are all quiet folk; but I don't know about his mother's side so well. I know this, however, that two first cousins of his mothers died in the asylum on the hill, and his blood must be tainted'.

However, this contradicted a statement made by Mrs Dyer. She stated that she knew Joseph Thomas, an uncle of Thomas's father, and that he was in the asylum because in her words. *'He is insane'.*

Corporal Lyons, a native of Lampeter, had been stationed in the orderly room at Carmarthen as a clerk. He had known Thomas from May 1892, when they were at the Mount Wise Barracks, Devonport. He described how Thomas had become a schoolmaster at the garrison of the Seventh Company Western Division, Royal Artillery. Corporal Lyons described Thomas as being quiet almost too quiet to be in the army. As a schoolmaster he earned 3s 3d a day of which 4½ was deducted leaving 2s 10½d a day spending money. To be a schoolmaster was no real promotion in point of rank, he was only equivalent to a bombardier. However, when his time with the colours was coming to an end Thomas had gone with the regiment to Fort Efford, Plymouth, he had started to drink heavily. After seven years in the regular army, Thomas passed out to the reserve in the August of 1893 and then returned to Carmarthen.

At the Magistrates Court
Thomas was brought before the borough bench on Monday 20th November 1893 at 11 o'clock. By now, the whole of Carmarthen had heard about the murder and the streets around the courthouse were full. When Thomas appeared under police escort the crowd shouted, *'Lynch him'* the police had to force a path into the court. As the waiting crowd outside heard news of the proceeding inside the crowded courtroom, many

started to bang on the doors, again shouting *'Lynch him'*. As the evidence was read out, Thomas appeared unaffected by the proceedings.

At the end of his appearance Thomas was heard to remark, *'I do not much care for this sort of thing'* (meaning the proceedings at the inquest), *'I will have to go there again tomorrow. Then I will have a rest and will only have to go there once again. Afterwards I expect I will have a long drop.'*

As Thomas appeared in the corridor of the court further cries of *'Lynch him, he ought to be murdered'* could be heard from the crowds in the Guildhall Square. The police had to force a path through the crowd and as Thomas passed through the portals of the Guildhall, the throng was so great that he had to be carried to the carriage waiting to convey him to the gaol. It was only with skill that the driver of the carriage was able to prevent the two horses from bolting or shying and crushing the spectators. The carriage entered Nott Square and up Queen Street before entering the prison gates, which by now, was under heavy guard.

Carmarthen Railway Station

The mother and father of Mary Jane Jones arrived at Carmarthen on the 2.56 p.m. train from Swansea. The father had heard the news early in the morning, having received a telegram saying that something had happened to his daughter. At that time, he had no idea of what was to come. The first indication he had was when he was passing a public house in Fforestfach. He heard some men talking about a murder in Carmarthen. He could not bear to read the account and could not even tell his wife of what he had heard. One of his sons was working at the face at Fforestfach colliery. He got word to the son but his son was unable to get up the bank in time to go with his parents. When they arrived in Carmarthen some relatives were waiting to take them to the mortuary and this was the first that the mother knew of why they were in Carmarthen. A more heart-rending scene could not be imagined than that of a man and woman of middle age shedding scolding tears of grief, weeping:

> *'I wish I was near to protect my dear little girl. I wish she had sent to tell me that this man was going after her. He had no right to go after my poor little daughter; she was to young. We have had enough trouble in the family lately, goodness knows, without this terrible stroke.'*

No words could describe the scene at the mortuary when the stricken parents hand in hand, viewed the mutilated body of their beloved child.

The Inquest

The inquest into the death of Mary Jane Jones took place on Tuesday 21st November 1893. A murderer presents himself as a curious figure to the ordinary man, and it was only natural that all the approach roads to the Guildhall were crowded by 11 o'clock when Thomas was due to appear for formal identification before the inquest.

Sergeant Jones gave his evidence and added one very significant and material point to the testimony that he had given at the magistrate's court on Monday. It was a remark made by Thomas:

'I did it because the girl would not have me'.

That undoubtedly is the explanation. Had Mary Jane accepted the advances made by Thomas, a man much older than her, she would have not been murdered. Her refusal infuriated him to the point of frenzy. He received the verdict of the inquest as if he was undergoing some pleasant ordeal. In this way, he differed from other local murderers. David Rees, (1888) the Llanelli murderer, who had assumed an air of complete innocence, and Henry Jones (1888), who had murdered his little daughter in Blue Street, Carmarthen by cutting her throat with a razor. Jones frequently broke into a paroxysm of grief and weeping. At his trial, he pleaded guilty but the judge Mr Justice Grantham advised him to plead not guilty. Jones said he could not, whereupon the judge addressed the council. The jury found him to be insane and he was sent to Broadmoor. But, George Thomas seems as careless of his terrible position and as indifferent to his fate as one could possible be.

The Funeral

Johnstown, presented a melancholy and depressing sight on the Wednesday morning before the funeral. The general gloominess of the town was still more marked by the dull sombre sky. Mary Jane's body had been taken to her Aunt Phillips house for the funeral. In the same road stood the house of her murderer. With the funeral service arranged for Thursday afternoon, it was to be a public affair with the internment at Llanllwch churchyard. The coffin was of polished oak trimmed with brass handles. The inscription read:

Mary Jane Jones
Died November 19, 1893
Aged sixteen years.

No doubt with the passing of time some rustic gravedigger has moved that piece of brass with his pick and shovel, not knowing what terrible truth lies behind the simple words-

Died November 19, 1893

Long before the funeral at 3 o'clock the cottage adjoining the Royal Oak, was crowded with the people from the town. Outside the crowds had swelled with hundreds of visitors to Carmarthen who had come to the fate and gala that was to take place on the same day. Mr Studt, the famous fairground proprietor was also in town. However, it was the funeral that took everyone's attention. The service was conducted in Welsh. From the house the procession proceeded to Llanllwch Church where Mary Jane Jones was laid to rest, a young girl who in the brightness and innocence of youth had met one of the most terrible of deaths.

Letters from the Murderer
On Tuesday 21st November, 1893, Thomas sent a letter to his parents. In Johnstown in one corner the initials appeared *'J.W.F.'*, Mr Forbes, the prison Governor had initialled the envelope. It was addressed to Mr John Thomas, 3, Job's Well, Johnstown, Carmarthen, South Wales:

'L P—C.4'
From George Thomas
H.M. Prison, Carmarthen
21st November, 1893

Dear Parents,
I can just imagine the surprise and sorrow with which you heard of my being here and the cause thereof, but dear parents, let me impress you not to grieve for me, as at present I am in pretty good spirits and hope that it will soon be all over. Should you wish to see me you can do so by applying at the prison gates; the visiting hours are 10 to 12 morning and 2 and 4 in the afternoon.

At present, I am to remain in my own clothes, so that at the end of work I shall need a change of underclothing. I am also allowed to obtain my food from home while I am awaiting trial, but I do not think I shall put you to any inconvenience in providing that for me, so for the present I conclude,

From your affectionate son
George Thomas

PS
I can receive one letter from you daily. Should you wish to write, my address will be H.M. Prison Carmarthen

H.M. Prison Carmarthen
23rd November, 1893

Dear Parents

Again, I write you these few lines, hoping this time my letter will meet with a reply, either in the form of a letter or a visit. I know that, that which I am here for has disgraces you all, but for all that, I hope that I am not beyond reconciliation, so that I pray of you not to defer it any longer. Come one of you to see me as soon as possible. I have already given you the hours laid down for visiting, so that you can have no excuse whatever. I would tell you that I have some particular news to tell you. Hoping I shall see one of you tomorrow without fail,

I remain your ungrateful son
G Thomas

The Cambrian reported that Thomas had written a number of letters to his parents and had not received a reply:

H.M. Prison Carmarthen
29th November, 1893

Dear Parents,

I am almost at a loss as to what to say to you. I have already written two letters to you, but have as yet received no answer to either. I thought, perhaps, that on first hearing the news you were completely prostrated and could not very well venture up on a visit; but now, dear parents, a fortnight has almost elapsed, and surely you (Phoebe) might at least pay me a visit; but I had almost forgotten that you might be required at home with poor father, who, Mary tells me has not been able to attend work since hearing of my fate. However, when opportunity occurs, I shall be delighted to see you. I have received a letter from Anne full of consolation and telling me that she has written to you, and that I may expect a visit from her. I have nothing particular to tell you at present, since that I am in fairly good health, hoping you are the same, so with kind love to you all, I conclude,

From your affectionate son
George Thomas

PS
Dear father,
I hope that you by now are beginning to recover from that fearful shock which affects me as much, if not more, than yourself. To think that I should have given you so much trouble in your grey hairs; but I suppose it is the will of the Almighty and I must meet my fate accordingly.

G Thomas

In another letter dated 4th December, Thomas wrote again pleading for a letter from his parents:

H.M. Prison Carmarthen
4th December, 1893

Dear Parents
I don't know what has become of you lately, as you don't seem to be able to write me a few lines. I am rather anxious to know how father is getting on, and whether he has been able to return to his daily duties yet. I suppose now that Dan is away you have no one to write. What about David John and Sarah Jane? Surely they should be able to write a few lines over night, take it to Dan, and I could receive it the next morning. Dear Parents. I am glad to tell you that I am enjoying good health at present, but am patiently awaiting my trial. Every day here seems a week. I have received a letter from Anne, but I should very much like to know Tom's address. You might be able to let me know in your next letter. Hoping to receive a few lines from you soon,

I remain you affectionate son
G Thomas

PS
Has any one been after my discharge documents from home yet? If so you might let me know (Phoebe) when you come to town next.

GT

His father never went to the gaol to visit his son but his stepmother did visit. During that visit, Thomas asked about the funeral of Mary Jane but not a word as to what had caused him to commit such a brutal murder. The only things that he asked his stepmother for were a change of clothing and an occasional newspaper. However, Mrs Thomas advised him that reading the Bible would be of more benefit to him now in his hour of need. Mr John Thomas returned to work at the Old Foundry where he had worked for 47 years. It is said that he had forged the bolts that where to send his son into eternity.

Sentence of Death

It was on Monday 20th January, 1894 that George Thomas stood in the dock before Mr Justice Kennedy, to answer the charge of murder. The Clerk of the court addressing him said; – *'George Thomas, do you understand English?'* He replied in an unfaltering voice *'Yes Sir'* and when the charge was put to him, he spoke in the same tone: *'Not Guilty sir'*.

The evidence before the court included that of Mr J.W. Forbes, Governor of H.M. Prison, at Carmarthen, – *'I have held the appointment of Governor for six years. Thomas was received into the prison on 20th November last. I saw every day with the exception of the days between 1st and 16th December, as I was on sick leave. He was perfectly calm and to all appearances rational. He is the most callous prisoner I have ever known, he is extremely so.'*

Dr Pringle gave evidence as to the mental state of Thomas and he concluded that insanity could lie dormant in some people if there is no cause to bring it out. He was of the opinion that Thomas was unable to form a rational judgement as to the moral character of his act. He stated that Thomas was suffering from Homicidal Monomania, a condition in which a person, without any adequate motive or reason, makes a sudden unreasoning attempt upon the life of another and that other being very often one who is near and dear. He ended his evidence by saying that homicidal mania is not consistent with self-control because ones judgement is defective and that the act of surrendering to the police in a cool manner was consistent with anyone suffering from Homicidal Monomania.

Dr Williams, the visiting surgeon to the prison also gave evidence. He stated that in his opinion, Thomas was sane and that he was a callous and indifferent to the murder and he drew the conclusion that, morally, he was very depraved. Dr Williams also stated that he could not find any indication of illusions or hallucinations. He formed the opinion that Thomas knew exactly what he was doing and that he had full control over his actions.

The jury had two theories to consider; one was that he was in full possession of his facilities to make himself responsible for the crime. On the other hand, the second theory that here was a man who was suffering homicidal monomania and that the rejection of his affections by the young woman was the spark that set the train on fire and woke up the latent maniac, resulting in the death of Mary Jane Jones.

When all the evidence had been put before the court the jury retired at

7 o'clock in the evening and after 39 minutes returned with the verdict 'Guilty *and Sane*'.

An official then placed the black cap on the Judge's head and in a hushed courtroom; Mr Justice Kennedy addressed Thomas:

> *'George Thomas, you have been found guilty of the awful crime of wilful murder by a jury that has most carefully and patiently heard the whole of the evidence in the case. It is not for me to add to that which must be the intensity of your feelings at this moment by long words of mine. I can only express the earnest hope that in such time as may elapse whilst you spend your allotted time on earth you may seek forgiveness for your sins where alone forgiveness of sin can be found. I must now pass upon you the sentence of the court, the only sentence which I can pass, and that is that you shall be taken hence to the place whence you came, and from thence to a legal place of execution. That you shall be hanged by the neck until you are dead, that your body be buried within the precincts of the prison wherein you shall last be confined after your conviction, and may the Lord have mercy on your soul.'*

Throughout the trial Thomas's expression was composed and unruffled, even, now when the jury had given their verdict or, still more harrowing, when the Judge pronounced the sentence of death, he did not exhibit the slightest trace of feeling or remorse. As the judge uttered the words *'And may the Lord have mercy on your soul'*, he made a left about face, as if on a parade square and disappeared to the cells below. Many in the square outside were in the windows of the surrounding houses and they were able to tell the waiting crowd the moment the judge put on his black cap, it was at this moment that the crowd gave way to their frustration and uttered a loud cheer.

The Execution
George Thomas was executed at Carmarthen Prison on 13th February, 1894 at 8 o'clock. From the moment he had surrendered to the police to the final snap of the rope, he had displayed a demeanour and a general behaviour described as being opposite to that of any man expecting execution. Whilst in the prison, he had been offered books such as, 'Pilgrims Progress' and 'The Life of Christ'. He never looked at them and spoke about religion in a satirical way. He frequently remarked to the warders, who were detailed to watch over him, when they stated that they believed in the Bible, *'How do you know it is true'*, and taunted the warders with being afraid of the hereafter. He evidently treated Christianity as superstition. When the High Sheriff told him that the

reprieve had failed, he simply said *'Very well'* and walked away in a huff. He slept and ate as if nothing was wrong. The governor even remarked, 'I never had one like him before'.

The executioner was to be Billington. He arrived on the London and North Western train at 3 o'clock on Monday 12th February. The crowds were out in force. As the train steamed into the station the crowd quickly scanned the passengers for the first sight of the famous executioner. He was soon spotted and the crowds converged on him, trying to question him, but he remained silent as he walked the short distance from the station to the gaol.

The scaffold had been prepared and tested by the prison but on the arrival of Billington he set about carrying out his own test. He placed a 155 lb sack of sand, the weight of Thomas, attached the rope, and tested the bolt. Over night, the sand remained in place to stretch the rope, only being removed two hours before the time set for the execution.

At a quarter to eight, the officials went to the central dome inside the prison where they could command a view of the condemned cell. Every detail was timed to the second as, almost at once Thomas came into view and the solemn tone of the prison bell rang out. It was now ten to eight. As if waiting for the bell, the Chaplain started to read the bible and the executioner pinioned Thomas. Billington spoke to Thomas and the procession formed. The Chaplain lead the procession reading the burial service, then came Mr Powell the Chief Warder, then the prisoner, walking with a firm gait, between two warders. The Governor, Sheriff, Surgeon, and other officials followed the executioner, who wore a black velvet skullcap. Thomas was so calm and collected that he noticed that Mr Powell was walking with a different step to himself. In a soldierly manner changed step to be in military form. The Chaplain walked over the trap to the other side of the room and Thomas quietly stepped onto the mark on the trap door. As he looked at his feet and with the Chaplain reciting, *'Of whom shall we seek for succour but thee, O Lord'*, Billington quickly pinioned his ankles and with the Chaplain still reciting, the cap was placed over Thomas's head and the rope positioned around the neck. With a nod from the executioner the Chaplain said *'Lord have mercy on my soul'*. With the lever pulled, Thomas dropped and in an instant was dead. A drop of 6 ft 6 inch had been given. The whole process had taken less than 60 seconds from the time that he had entered the execution shed.

The gallows had been built seven years before and Mr John Thomas, the father of the condemned man, had forged the bolt used to activate the trap door in the Old Foundry at Carmarthen some years before.

Billington left the prison and caught the 10.30 train bound for Manchester.

Thomas Richards   29th November, 1894

'It was on a Saturday morning that Thomas Richards, a 41-year-old sailor, appeared before Carmarthen Assizes charged with the wilful murder of his sister-in-law Mary Davies of Borth, sometime between 20th and the 21st September, 1894. At the time the precincts of the Guildhall was crowded with an eager crowd waiting for the court doors to open. By 9.30, the jury were in place and awaiting the arrival of the Judge Mr Justice Lawrence. With the arrival of the judge, the warders brought the prisoner from the cells below and the court fell into silence at his appearance. He appeared to be very sickly and despondent. With the charge read out, he replied in a quiet voice "Not Guilty".'

The Carmarthen Journal, 1894.

It appeared that Mary Davies's husband, a sailor, was also a close friend of Richards and on the morning of 20th September James Davies was leaving Swansea Harbour just as Richards was arriving in port. Richards had asked his captain for four days leave of absence to attend Swansea Hospital. This was not the case. He travelled to Aberystwyth arriving between 10 and 11 in the evening, and then stealing a horse from a field. He made his way to Borth, a distance of some nine miles and made straight to his sister-in-laws house.

He broke into the house and ransacked the downstairs but as he ascended the stairs Mary Davies lit a candle and started to scream. Richards's placed a pillow over her face to smother her screams and left her for dead. At first, she was not missed as she was a seamstress and was often away from home for a few days at a time. However, as the weekend drew near, neighbours became suspicious, entered the house, and found the body of Mary on the bed with the pillow covering her face. At first, there was no suspicion of foul play. It was not until the discovery of a five-pound note on the floor of Richard's by his son that suspicion fell on him. It appeared that the National Provincial Bank in Aberystwyth had handed over £62.11s.7d to a man who had signed his name as James Davies. Richards had stolen a deposit note from the house and had forged the name James Davies to obtain the money. He had asked the bank to cash the deposit note that contained £262.4s.8d and to place £200 in another account, leaving him with £62.4s.8d plus the interest. He then placed £40 in a tin and mailed this to his wife and the new deposit note back to Mary's house. A witness was produced stating that Richards had been in the Skinners Arms at Aberystwyth and that he had asked the landlady to write two envelopes for him, one of which was addressed to Mary Davies and the other to Mrs Richards.

After a search that lasted several days Thomas Richards was arrested at the Falcon Inn, Old Market Street Neath, on suspicion of robbery at Borth and immediately said, *'I know nothing about it'*. At the police station he was searched and a watch, £7.8s.5½ and a gold wedding ring were found in his pocket. He protested his innocence, and stated that he had not been in Aberystwyth for over 12 months and demanded to know with what evidence they were charging him. He was charged with the death of Mary Davies, at Borth on 20th September, 1894 and with breaking into the house on the same night, and stealing a deposit note to the value of £263 and a £5 Bank of England note and with forging the name of James Davies at the National Provincial Bank Aberystwyth and obtaining £62.11s.8d by deception. He denied all the charges, saying that the witnesses were wrong.

The ring proved to be the most damning evidence. John Davies, Mary's husband, was able to identify the ring and said that his wife would never remove it from her finger. When the coroner had seen the body he noticed that a ring had been recently removed from the dead woman's hand. The evidence against Richards was conclusive.

At first, Richards denied that he had been in Borth, saying that he had gone to Neath from Swansea having just returned from France in a vessel called the Dorset and that he had bought the ring some 3 years before. He said he paid 30 shillings for it. He denied being in Aberystwyth in the previous twelve months. When he was confronted with the evidence of the landlady of The Skinners Arms and the bank teller he broke down and said *'Oh dear, I don't know what came over me'*.

Richards made a confession to the police as he was being transported from Neath to Aberystwyth.

Statement made to Police when arrested:

'I wish to tell you all as far as I can remember. I came to Aberystwyth by the last train on Thursday night last and then went onto Borth. On the way I turned into a field, caught a pony, which I rode to near Borth. I left the pony near Borth and went onto my sister-in-law's house and got in through a window, which I opened with a gimlet [a small boring tool]. After I got in I lighted some matches and found some keys on a chest of drawers and took from one of them two notes, I then went upstairs, where my sister-in-law slept, who, by that time, had lighted a candle. She was then screaming, and in order to prevent her, I pushed her on the bed and placed a pillow over her head. I never thought of killing her, I only wanted to prevent her from screaming. I did not know she was dead until you told me at Neath. (Chief Constable of Cardiganshire, Mr Howell Evans). I left the house through the front door, and went onto Aberystwyth. On my way, I passed my own house, and pushed the note (£5) under the door. I had been drinking heavily, and did not know what I was doing. I must have been mad.'

Reported in the Carmarthen Journal

On his return to Aberystwyth, Richards was further charged with removing the ring from Mary Davies's finger. This he denied. It was not until 2nd October that Richards sent for the Chief Constable. He then confessed to stealing the ring from the dresser. He denied that he had removed the ring from the dead woman's finger:

'*I had no intention of taking her life, and if I did, I hope the Lord will forgive me.*'

At his trial, Richards continued to protest his innocence despite the witnesses who saw him in Aberystwyth and Borth before and after the murder. The jury took one hour to return a verdict of guilty.

With that the Judge donned the black cap and addressed Richards:

'*The jury, after a long patient, and exhausting trial, have found you guilty of the crime of murder, and I always think it right, and I think it is the least that the jury can ask of the presiding Judge, that when he agrees he should express that agreement publicly. I think there is no other conclusion, which could be rightly come to except that verdict which the jury have given on the present occasion. That you were the means by which this unhappy woman lost her life I think no one can have any possible doubt. You were there for the purpose of taking valuable property in any case, and there can be no doubt whatever that you chose a time when you knew that the husband had gone to sea, and that you did all that you possible could to hide the result of your crime. Maybe, I do not know; it is a matter only as far as your mind is concerned; you knew when you left that house whether that woman was dead or not. Undoubtedly the whole of the evidence shows that there can be no doubt whatever that her death was due to violence used by you, and ask you earnestly that during such time as may be left to you, to make your peace with that God against whose laws you have so grievously offended. The only duty that I have now to discharge is to pass sentence upon you in the terms which I am obliged to pass by law; and that sentence is that you be taken from hence to the place from whence you came, and from there hanged by the neck until you shall be dead and that your body be afterwards buried within the precincts of the prison in which you shall be last confined after your conviction. And may the Lord have mercy on your soul.'*

The Carmarthen Journal 1894

Richards turned pale as he walked to the cells below the court. In a later interview in the cells at Carmarthen Gaol with his solicitor, he commented that he thought *'the Judge was a bit hard on me.'*

Richards's wife and son visited him at the gaol a few days before the execution and the Governor and the warders present described the scene was as being terribly touching. They all cried bitterly but it was the son's mournful sound that was the most heart rendering, a sound that was heard throughout the gaol. It was the last meeting and parting of a husband and wife, and the final farewell of an affectionate son before the executioner arrived to carry out the extreme penalty of the law. It was shortly after the visit by the family that the High Sheriff arrived at the Gaol and informed Richards that the date of execution had been set for 29th November.

During his incarceration, Thomas Richards resigned himself to his fate, as much as it is possible to imagine a man in his position to be. Nevertheless, as the final day approached he presented to the prison authorities a final statement:

'I don't remember leaving Swansea or how I left there. The first place I remember was Pencader, when I asked if I could have a drink, and I am not sure whether I had one or not. The next place I remember was Aberystwyth Station, and I think I went out straight. I don't remember going into the Railway Inn, but I won't swear I went in. this was after ten o'clock. Very few can tell I am drunk until they speak to me, as drink does not affect my walk very much. The next time I remember anything was turning into a field, and I have a indistinct recollection of catching a pony. The pony was a fresh one. I had not ridden for many years, and I had no reins. I don't know how I got out of the field. I can remember going through with my arms around the pony, and when near Brynbala I let go my arm and fell on my back. I then passed my own house, but just by the board school, something came to my mind and told me to go to my sister-in-laws house to fetch money. I knew she had

money, and had an idea where she kept it. That is where her mother kept it when I lived there for two years immediately after we were married. I thought she kept it in the small drawer at the top of the chest of drawers on the left hand. I went there and did not go near my own house. I saw nobody about. When I got to the deceased house, I tried the window first, and found there was no bolt. I lifted the window right up and went in. I am positive of this. Although I am reminded of the gimlet hole in the back door, I know nothing of the gimlet or the back door. After going in I began to look for the drawer. I lit a match, and found the door locked, and I saw keys on the top of the chest immediately above the drawer. The ring was also there. I took the ring and opened the door. I found the deposit note and a £5 note. This took me about five minutes. The door of the parlour was open. I then went upstairs, and, as I was upstairs, I heard her strike a match. I went forward to the bedroom, and saw the deceased with one foot out of the bed-I think it was the left. She had not got wholly out of bed. When she saw me she screamed once, and I gave her a small push on the breast, which caused her to fall on the bed, and I then threw the pillow on her face with one hand to prevent her screaming. No unnecessary violence was used in any way, and all I thought was to get away. I was then anxious to get out, and I believe I blew the candle out and went down stairs and out through the front door. I had put the window down when I first went in. I was there a moment. I did nothing to her in anyway indecent, nor had I ever done anything to her. I did not do anything to her except as I have said, and did not intend to harm her in any way, as I had no cause to do anything to her. I am innocent of any intention of doing her any harm. I think I heard her scream as I went through the front door, but not much. I did not know she was dead until the Chief Constable of Cardiganshire told me on Wednesday. I was only in the house a little over 5 minutes. There was no struggle at all except as I have said. I have said all that has taken place. I said nothing to her and she said nothing to me, as when she began to scream I was afraid somebody would hear and rouse the village up. I left the keys in the same place as I had found them, unless I left them in the lock. I took nothing away except the ring, the deposit note, and the £5 note. I don't know what possessed me to take them. After leaving, I went up to my own house and put the £5 note under the front door of my wife's house. I had no gimlet, and have no recollection of any such thing. I don't know why I didn't go into the house. I heard the clock strike two when I was doing this. I then left for Aberystwyth, and when I got to Moelcerni I went into a field and slept until daylight, when I proceeded to Aberystwyth. I first went to the Skinners Arms about eight o'clock and had several beers there. Miss Ellis's story is true as to what took place. I admit every thing that the witnesses say to the money, but I most emphatically deny the murder. I don't know why I took the £64. I sent the deceased the note for £200 on the

Friday morning. I admit all the witnesses say as to what took place on Saturday. I do not remember saying anything about the ring, as I was drinking hard the whole time. I stayed at the Royal Oak until the Monday, when I left for Llanelli, and there saw Peake, but I do not remember what I said, as I was muddled. I bought shoes there and I also bought fowls from there, and that is all I remember, I was drinking hard there. I do not remember that I said anything about the ring. From Llanelli I went to Neath about seven o'clock, and went to the Falcon until I was arrested. I do not know what I said when arrested, and it may be what the police say is true. When I first saw the Chief, he said in Welsh that he charged me with three things, breaking in the house, stealing the money, and causing her death. I do not remember what I said 'they are mistaken'. I was completely overcome when he told me she was dead, and I hardly knew what I said as to Pugh's evidence. My recollection is that I went to the bank, produced the note, and told him how much I wanted and he asked me to sign. I did so, 'J.D.' He did not ask me to sign my own name. When I was on board the Coquette, captained by Captain Jenkins, Havelock Villa, Aberystwyth, in the west coast of Africa, I got a fever, which affected my joints and head. I was never in my mind. All I thought was to get the money, and when I considered that, they would find the money gone. I sent my wife £40, as I knew she would not use it, and it would be there for the deceased. I did not know that she was dead until the chief told me at Neath. Before my God I say I never intended her any injury or to murder her. I had got the money before I went upstairs. I don't know what possessed me to go upstairs, unless it was to talk to her in my silliness. She used to sleep in the parlour where the money was kept. I don't know whether she recognised me. I did not touch her body anywhere, except on her chest with my own hand. I did not touch her face or thigh – did not touch her clothing, in fact, did not touch her at all, except as I have said. When I touch her I used the left hand, which had the effect of making her lie across the bed, and I took up the pillow with the right. I did not intend to strangle her, and only meant to stop her, for I put out the candle the same time. We had no struggle in any way. I have only come to myself since I have been in custody. I am nearly broken-hearted at what has happened.
Signed
Thomas Richards.'

The Home Secretary stated that he could see no reason why he should interfere with the carrying out of the extreme penalty of the law. Richards appeared to accept his fate. He even expressed to his warder that he believed that the sentence passed upon him was a merciful divine decree.

The arrival of James Billington in the town from Manchester on the Wednesday caused a sensation. Despite the fact that he had officiated at the execution of George Thomas in the previous February, the town folk were keen to see the famous executioner and followed him from the railway station to the gaol. When admitted into prison Richards had weighed 136 lbs, but when weighed on the Wednesday he had gained 12 lbs and now weighed 148 lbs.

Billington allowed a drop of 7 feet, and a weighted sack filled with sand to Richards's weight of 148 lbs attached to the executioner's rope in order to stretch the rope overnight. It was at two minutes to eight that Billington entered the cell and pinioned Richards. The condemned man made no comment, and walked unaided to the platform. He had made up his mind to die. With the rope secured around his neck, the clock struck eight and the lever was pulled Richards fell to his death. It had only taken two minutes from the entry to the cell to the hoisting of the black flag.

Richards was buried fully dressed in quick lime during the course of the morning, within the prison walls. With the customary notice pinned to the prison gate signalled the end of Thomas Richards the Borth murderer.

Chapter 6

Carmarthen Gaol to be Closed

It was on 13th February, 1922 that the people of Carmarthen found that their historic gaol was to close. The government had set up a committee headed by Sir Eric Geddes with the purpose of saving expenditure in all departments. Docks, Board of Health, Mines, Police and Prison, throughout England and Wales, none were spared from a government proposing to save in excess of £75 million.

Sir Eric Geddes carried the axe to all corners of the Principality. The Western Mail carried the above heading and carried the report:

'The Home Office has issued an intimation that it proposes to close His Majesty's Prison, Carmarthen, as from the end of March.

This step is believed to be in accord with the present campaign to affect economies in the national expenditure as urged in the Geddes Report. Eight other prisons in the country, it is learned, are also to be closed.

The Geddes Committee report states regarding the closing of prisons (England and Wales): We understand that the Prison Commission are of the opinion that no further closing of prisons is considered to be practicable at the present, but in view of the release of Sinn Fein prisoners we think this question should be very carefully examined.'

The Western Mail
13th February, 1922

At the time Carmarthen, prison served the three counties of Carmarthen, Pembroke and Cardigan. In addition to the Governor, it had a staff of twelve warders. It had played a major role in the history of the town and surrounding County, from the early days of the public executions, the last being in 1829 (David Evans). Crowds had flocked to these occasions for their *'Roman Holiday'*, to watch and stare at the poor retch being put on display for their pleasure and gratification once sent into eternity the crowds still came for a free view of the body before it was drawn and quartered. When the executions were moved within the prison grounds and away from the public gaze, only the select few attended to witness the event. (Thomas Richards 1894).

The day following the announcement of Carmarthen's closure Swansea prison announced that all of its female prisoners were to be transferred to Cardiff, making way for the prisoners from Carmarthen gaol. There is little doubt that if the prison had not closed, the county and the walls of Carmarthen gaol would have witnessed more executions.

With the transfer of prisoners to Swansea Prison, the executions in Carmarthen ended. Many had been incarcerated within the walls, from the early Rebecca riots in 1843 to the children of the town whose only crime was to steal to survive. Executions continued in the country for another hundred years, but for Carmarthen the axe was about to fall and Sir Eric Geddes was about to wield that axe.

With Caernarfon and Usk (Usk reopened as a borstal in 1939) under threat of closure and Ruthin Prison closed during the First World War, only Swansea and Cardiff were left to serve the whole of the principality. At the time, the report caused considerable bad feeling in Carmarthen. It was felt that the prison was the best situated for receiving prisoners from the West and Mid Counties and much inconvenience would be caused with the families and prisoners having to travel to Swansea and Cardiff.

With the closure about to hit many of the major industries in the Country many newspapers carried cartoons of Sir Eric Geddes, the Axe man. In February 1922, the people of Sheffield presented an axe of the finest Sheffield Steel to Sir Eric Geddes with the inscription:

'Dreadnaught and drive well home
The Old country is behind you,
And beneath you
This axe is made of the best
Sheffield Steel, and its edge is guaranteed
Against any nail any wood may contain'

The axe was trade marked with the word 'PAX'
And a laurel wreath as well as the inscription 'Made in Sheffield' was stamped on it.

One newspaper report of the time carried the report that Sir Eric Geddes was not going to speak in Parliament on his report as he had made plans on completion of his task to go to the Pyrenees. Only one prison in Wales facing closure received a reprieve and that was USK. In

March 1922, Carmarthen Gaol finally closed it was demolished in 1938 to make way for the new County Hall. In so doing, Sir Eric Geddes achieved in 1922 at Carmarthen what Nash and all the others before had failed to do and that was to destroy one of the most historic landmarks of West Wales.

A Final Twist in History

The gates to the prison went missing after the closure of the gaol and for over 70 years, their disappearance remained a mystery. The gates that were once securely locked to keep the prisoners in gaol returned to Carmarthen museum and are now left open for all to see and walk through. The last Governor of the gaol Captain John Nicholas had removed the 12-foot gates to adorn his countryseat, Maes Teilo, near Llandeilo. Maes Teilo, now a nursing home, returned the gates to Carmarthen, it was felt that gaol gates would not be an appropriate entrance to the nursing home.

History had come full circle.

Source of Reference

Books

For Whom The Bell Tolls, A century of executions, by Peter J R Goodall (Gomer Press 2001)
The Journal of the Welsh Bibliographical Society 1933
Response to Revolution by D O Thomas 1989
The Dictionary of Welsh Biography, Down to 1940
The Caermarthenshire Miscellany 1892
Carmarthen and its Neighbourhood William Spurrell 1879
Four Cheers for Carmarthen, The other side of the Coin Pat Molloy (Gomer Press 1981)
The Hangman's Record 1868-1899, Vol 1 by Steve Fielding (Chancery Press,1994)
Lord High Executioner by Howard Engel (Robson Books 1996)

Newspapers

The Cambrian
The South Wales Daily Post
The South Wales Evening Post
The Western Mail
The Carmarthen Journal